YOU CAN'T DO BUSINESS WITH HITLER

You Can't Do Business with Hitler

by DOUGLAS MILLER

AN ATLANTIC MONTHLY PRESS
BOOK

BOSTON
LITTLE, BROWN AND COMPANY
1941

Published June 1941
Reprinted June 1941 (twice)
Reprinted July 1941 (five times)

ATLANTIC—LITTLE, BROWN BOOKS
ARE PUBLISHED BY
THE ATLANTIC MONTHLY PRESS
IN ASSOCIATION WITH
LITTLE, BROWN AND COMPANY

PRINTED IN THE UNITED STATES OF AMERICA

Preface

A GREAT deal has been and is being written and spoken about fighting the Nazis or dealing with them. But there is one group in America which has not been adequately brought face to face with the facts. I mean American business men. Because I have spent fifteen years in their service at the United States Embassy in Berlin — six of them under the Nazi regime — I think I am in a position to do some plain speaking on this subject. I believe that what we do *now* will determine our economic history for years to come. And I believe that what affects the American business man cannot help but affect every American.

D. M.

Denver, May 12, 1941

CHAPTER I
NAZI AIMS AND METHODS

1. Hitler Is Our Enemy

IF Hitler can defeat Britain, he has removed the last obstacle to his effective control over Europe, Africa, and Asia Minor. The Nazis will then be able to construct a scientific slave state in which they retain for themselves all possibilities of military action, all control over important industrial operations, and in which they will be able to achieve a complete monopoly of scientific and technical knowledge. By these methods they can reduce the conquered peoples to entire helplessness; they can destroy rebellious groups; they can monopolize the entire resources of this great area and the man power of hundreds of millions of white, black, and brown slaves to carry on their designs in other parts of the world.

The Nazis will control the oceans. They will soon force a considerable part of South America into their economic orbit. We cannot overlook the possibility that they may secure a working agreement with the Soviet Union and the Japanese new order in Asia for a terrific assault upon us. They will be able to turn to their advantage our need for foreign markets, our lack of certain critical raw materials. They can exert pressure upon American property in the territories which they control. They can project fear into the hearts of millions of Americans through relatives and friends in the Old World. They can and will use the device of a centralized economic system, buying and selling for half the world, to put pressure upon our economy at many points.

They will have the assistance of numerous agents throughout North America, some of them moved by racial consciousness, some bribed by propaganda funds, and some despairing of democracy's continued existence in a totalitarian world. The Nazis hate the United States more poisonously than any other country. Our very existence disproves their racial and economic theories. We have welcomed their beaten enemies. We persist in speaking, printing, and broadcasting disagreeable truths which they would like to see suppressed. Above all, we alone possess the loot which would make a world conquest worth while.

Nazi Aims and Methods

The Nazis have often said that there are two opposite poles in the world: Germany, the pole of order, discipline, and scientific progress; and the United States, the pole of democratic anarchy, decadent Christianity, and the degeneration and loss of efficiency which accompanies a system of free enterprise. Hitler's conquest is only partial and incomplete until we are brought into his world system.

I make these statements on the basis of my long residence in Berlin, my close association with Nazi leaders and their party, a detailed study of National Socialist books, pamphlets, and newspapers from the very beginning of their movement when they were less cautious about discussing ultimate objectives. These convictions I formed slowly under the pressure of overwhelming evidence.

One and a half years before Hitler assumed power, that is in October 1931, I prepared a report to Washington of how the coming National Socialist State in Germany would operate. This account still stands substantially correct. Several years before the outbreak of the present war I had arrived at the belief that war was coming and that further commercial relations between

Germany and the United States would come to an end. Accordingly, on September 1, 1938, I cabled a request to return to the United States, which later was acted upon. In the American press I foretold that war was imminent in the summer of 1939. I believe that this record entitles me to make public some of my experiences with the Nazis and — after drawing conclusions from them, discussing Nazi aims and methods — to project existing Nazi policy into the future and describe what sort of world we shall have to live in if Hitler wins.

2. *Rule of Force Not Law*

What does Nazi Germany stand for? [First, for the principle of force instead of law. The Nazis have so little respect for written law that they have not even bothered to abolish the previous Weimar Constitution.] It still continues to operate in part. For example, the German post offices, city fire departments, and the tax collectors work on just about the same legal basis as before. What has changed is the fact that the individual has no basic civil rights now. German

6

courts are instructed to decide cases not purely upon written law, but according to "healthy public opinion." Since such opinion is not recorded anywhere, this means in practice the judge's opinion at the time, and the judge is a Nazi functionary. [No firm or individual has any rights which the government is bound to respect.]

[Under this situation the distinction between capitalism and socialism disappears. There is no point in discussing whether Germany is socialistic because all capital is at the immediate disposal of the government. Hitler rightly believes that he has restored the "Primacy of Politics." When a man's life is a forfeit at the whim of government officials, it makes no difference whether he has title to his property or not. In this way the Nazis have extended their control over German economy without the necessity of creating a new body of rules or party dogmas.] They move straight ahead, right to their objectives, without having to worry about maintaining the party line or conforming to any particular economic creed. The government does not need to confiscate the property of large industrial firms. An official needs only to suggest that a gift of a certain sum would be in order and the hint does not need to be made twice. Even such industrial giants as Krupp and the United Steel Works readily acted on the suggestion that they turn over some of their most valuable coal mines and ore properties to the official Hermann Goering works without any compensation except almost worthless stock.

An American company operated a large plant in the Rheinland. They told me that they had made heavy shipments of equipment from their German factories to Brazil. It so happened that Brazil, like Germany, had exchange restrictions in force, so that money owed for these shipments was not allowed to be sent from Brazil to Germany. The American company, however, was rather pleased to have spread their risk and got material out of Germany into Brazil, which, after all, was closer to the United States.

One morning early I had an urgent telephone call from the firm, stating that their American officials were all on their way to Berlin by plane and wanted me to arrange an interview with the Consul-General immediately. When they arrived, we found that the German government had given them two weeks to get into Germany the money covering their shipments to Brazil or else every one of the Americans in the firm would be put into jail. After considerable negotiation, the parent company in the United States was forced to send a very large sum to Germany to cover these shipments and now has the money tied up in both Brazil and Germany.

The German manager of an American hardware company used to visit me in Berlin, traveling clear across the country to do so, because he said there was no one in his vicinity that he could tell his troubles to except his wife. His firm had piled up profits for several years in German marks; and now they were under pressure from the Nazis, who wanted this money to build low-cost houses for Nazis living in the neighborhood — a project which even the Nazis estimated would bring in only about 1 per cent a year on the invested capital. Of course, his home office cabled "No," but his local German Board of Directors, his company treasurer and auditor, insisted that this must be done, or trouble was sure to follow. The poor man was an outcast in his own plant.

American firms in Germany which manu-

9

factured special equipment suitable for the army and the National Socialist Party have been practically taken over by the authorities to work on such products. A large American company owns a plant in Berlin which is now making such articles as tiny hidden microphones to be placed in ordinary telephone receivers and connected with the office of the Secret Police, and small portable television sending apparatus operated by foot pedals like a bicycle and suitable for operation in front-line trenches, so they can televise to the rear the image received by the lens of a periscope projecting above the top of the trench. When the president of the American company and other American representatives visited Berlin, they were not even allowed to enter the plant which they were nominally supposed to own. Of course, they had to keep on paying taxes, but this was about the limit of their connection with the enterprise.

An American typewriter company owns a subsidiary in Germany which manufactures office equipment. This firm has long been a competitor of the German-owned Continental Typewriter. The Ministry of Economics set up Commodity Committees to make restrictions in foreign trade and in production quotas. The Chairman of the Committee on office equipment was the head of the Continental firm. Accordingly, when the American representative visited the German Ministry of Economics, he was told that his German subsidiary would be given no export subsidy or other official support, such as was enjoyed by his competitors. Finally, the officials became very frank and told him, "We think there are too many typewriter manufacturers in Germany, and you had better get out of business. We are going to make regulations increasingly stiff for you until you fall into line. For one thing, we have a shortage of skilled labor, and some of your employees are needed in the factory of the Continental Company. The sooner you close your plant, the better for you." Nobody, however, mentioned any payment for the money invested by the Americans in their German enterprise.

3. *Leadership Principle*

Another important element in Nazi policy is the leadership principle. All power is inherent in the person of Fuehrer Adolf Hitler. He may delegate a limited power to sub-Fuehrers and so on down the line. The affirmation or assent of the public is not necessary. True, Hitler did promise to hold a popular election at least once a year which should ratify his important decisions. This promise has been disregarded now since the annexation of Austria. A large and almost unanimous vote was, in fact, secured in support of the Nazi plans at every election held. Various methods were used to secure such favorable returns, the principal one being as follows: —

Although the institution of the closed polling booth was still maintained, large signs were placed at the polling places which read, "Patriotic Germans are proud to show how they vote." Ballots were marked accordingly at an open table with the Secret Police looking on. There was no place on the ballot for a vote of "No." The only way to show dissension was to mutilate the ballot. In case such methods do not produce 100 per cent results, there is no doubt that Dr. Goebbels is perfectly prepared to supply the required election figures as needed. In fact in some German elections there were more "Yes" votes recorded in certain areas than the number of voters in residence.

In business enterprises a leader is responsible for each undertaking. In the Labor Front, the one great government union, there is no such procedure as voting by members. All decisions are made by the leader, Dr. Ley. Hitler believes there is only one policy, the right policy, and that this is known to the leader and that any questioning or complaining from the followers amounts to treason and leads to anarchy.

[In the Nazi state the individual is coming more and more to occupy a particular status in life which has been prepared for him, and he makes fewer independent decisions of his own. This is a return to the medieval conception of society. It virtually places the entire population in servitude.] As an illustration, take the hereditary peasantry who make up the bulk of Germany's farmers. These farmers are tied to the land. They cannot leave it; they cannot mortgage their property and crops. The eldest son of the farmer must carry on with the farm. He must support the younger brothers and sisters as long as they continue to reside at home. A farm boy can only marry a farm girl and vice versa. There has already been considerable agitation for the introduction of hereditary artisans, so that a barber's son must always remain a barber and presumably marry a barber's daughter, but the development has not gone this far yet. Undoubtedly the tendency is towards an introduction of standardized living; for the regimentation of every class of society.

[Hitler teaches that animals obey their individual instincts and impulses; but that when human beings form themselves into an ordered society, they must adopt common aims. As human society improves, it must become more ordered; and finally, if it is to be truly scientific, must subject itself to a single will — the will of the Fuehrer. He is always right. Hitler believes that in this way he can move eighty million Germans in a solid block, all marching in step — a tremendous mass maneuver, able to crash through the feeble resistance of ineffectual democracies who waste time in debate and whose absurd tolerance of individual wishes keeps them forever in a state of anarchy. To Hitler, the individual is similar to a single cell in our bodies, with no significant life of its own, but only useful as part of a greater whole — the race or the

14

state. National Socialism is really a reaction against modern civilization, which has become too complex for people with lazy minds.]

A German professor named Oswald Spengler wrote a book about this tendency, which he published in the year 1918 and called *The Decline of the West*. Spengler says at the close of his book, "The democratic nations must disappear, because they put their trust in illusions, more particularly the illusions of truth and justice. There is only one reality in the world — force. If you listen closely, you can already hear the tramp of the Caesars who are coming to take over the world." Now in 1941 the Caesars are here. The names of some of them are Hitler and Mussolini. They believe in force alone. They repudiate the idea of truth for its own sake. To them, truth is what will help their cause, and it changes every day according to their pleasure.

They do not believe in justice or fair dealing. In my office in Berlin, I used to keep framed on the wall a motto taken from an editorial in Hitler's newspaper, the *Voelkischer Beobachter* (Popular Observer), of August 3, 1936, which read like this: ["Justice and good nature should be limited to one's own people."] I used to look at this motto from time to time, just so as not to forget that the Nazis did not intend to treat us with justice; and it was useless to expect them to.

The totalitarians do not believe in mercy or pity or humanitarianism. They are profoundly selfish. They regard British and American conventionalized standards of conduct as pure hypocrisy, and they pride themselves on being realists who can face the facts. After several years' experience of living in a realist atmosphere, I confess a preference for a little civilized hypocrisy once in a while, to conceal some of the ugliness of the world. If we cannot always act according to the highest standards of ethics, the least we can do is to be ashamed of ourselves and conceal our shortcomings as much as possible. Such hypocrisy is much better than openly wallowing in evil and claiming that this is an honest and natural way to live.

Nazism, as I see it, meant that the German people became tired of beggary and turned to crime on a world scale. Some of us still remember the Ten Commandments we used to learn in Sunday School. As I run them over in my mind, it seems that the Nazis flagrantly violate all ten of them as a matter of common practice.

16

Nazi Aims and Methods

Murder, theft, lying, covetousness, are daily practices in totalitarian states; but in place of the old Ten Commandments, a new set has come into being. They might run like this: —

1. Thou shalt not marry a foreigner or have any partly foreign children.
2. Thou shalt not sell any holy German land to a foreigner.
3. Thou shalt not give any business secrets to a foreigner or sell him any valuable patent or trademark or piece of machinery.
4. Thou shalt not buy any foreign goods if German goods are available.
5. Thou shalt pay no debts to foreigners.
6. Thou shalt report to the proper authorities any information of military usefulness.
7. Thou shalt betray thy father, mother, or other members of the family to the Party, if they have uttered any treasonable sentiments.
8. Thou shalt place a picture or bust of Hitler in thy best room and place lighted candles or fresh flowers before it.
9. Thou shalt constantly attack and destroy all manifestations of civilization, such as art, literature, religion, science, education, law, good taste, good manners, and even correct grammar.
10. Thou shalt place the interests of the race, the Party, and the Fuehrer before everything else in the world.

4. Militarism

[Another feature of Nazi economy is the control of civil life by the military. For some years now the General Staff of the army has had the chief authority in the Ministry of Economics, while the Four-Year Plan with its new developments is practically a military operation throughout. This feature of Germany's economic life is not new. The people almost instinctively subordinate peacetime affairs to war necessities. Peace is not an end in itself, but merely a period of preparation for the next war] As long ago as 1924 I was visiting a newly erected plant for making agricultural machines near Halberstadt. My guide said, "Did you notice the size of the doors of this factory?" I did. They made up one whole side of the building. He explained that the plant was really designed to make warplanes and that the doors had to be large for that reason, also that the potato patch in which the factory was now situated had been chosen because it would make a fine landing field. The interesting thing about this anecdote is the fact that the government and army at that time had nothing to do with this situation. German private capitalists had decided to invest their inflationary profits in such ventures, and were patriotic enough to make all necessary provisions for the coming war. The German people did not have to be forced into military preparation — they prepared spontaneously.

A few years ago an important Nazi railroad official visited the United States. Upon his return to Germany, he gave me an interview and remarked about the strange manner in which railroad passenger cars were constructed here. I failed to understand his meaning. "Why, it's the way you build your passenger cars with a door at both ends and a right-angle turn in the vestibule before you can enter the car itself. How in the world would you ever evacuate the wounded from a big battlefield with that type of railroad equipment? In Germany we insist that a large number of passenger coaches be built with the doors at the side so that stretcher cases may be brought straight in and laid down without turning a corner." I confessed that I had never thought of this point, and I suppose most railroad men in America are in the same fix — but the Germans have been thinking about it. That is the reason why German automotive trucks are built with three axles, so that they may go over plowed fields or over shell-torn country in time of war. For the same reason the bumpers on German railroad cars were changed in design because the new type of bumper could be made on a machine that also makes artillery shells. This traditional flavor of military planning has been strengthened to all-devouring fanaticism under the Nazis. They have even taken soldiers whose blood belongs to the same group and placed them together in the same company so that blood transfusions can be arranged more quickly between comrades.

We can be sure that one purpose will pervade all German trade and economic policy after the war — namely, Germany's military advantage. As far back as the beginning of 1937, the administration of the Four-Year Plan and the Ministry of Economics was turned over to representatives of the General Staff. Three colonels, who were afterwards promoted to generals, started taking over the most important branches of German trade and industry at that time. Von Loeb, now reported dead, was given control of petroleum, nonferrous metals, and chemicals.

Von Hanneken was put in charge of iron and steel, and Von Jawitz was given the Administration of Foreign Trade and Foreign Exchange. Even in peacetime, the army General Staff controlled industry and trade. Even in peacetime, blockade experts were appointed in every important ministry to correlate its activities in such a way that Germany could become blockade-proof. It is not to be supposed that any other consideration will have more weight in postwar years than General Staff policy. It need not be expected that army control of industry and trade can be anything else than narrow-minded. It has one great advantage over control by Nazi Party officials — it is more honest.

The outbreak of war in September 1939 came just in time to postpone tremendous changes in German industrial organization. It was planned to segregate important industrial leadership and control into a number of great government-operated trusts, roughly similar to the Soviet trusts, with complete power in their respective fields. One benefit to be expected was efficiency obtained through standardization of equipment, machinery, and parts. Each great industrial group was to have a Fuehrer, subordinate, of course, to

the Super-Fuehrer, "Adolf." Three of these
persons were named: an army colonel with the
appropriate name of Von Schell was to administer
the automotive industry; Todt of Siegfried Line
fame was to be the Fuehrer of the Building
Trade; and a leading member of the Society of
German Engineers was to head the Machinery
Industry.

The Nazis planned first to standardize in the
automotive field. They expected to reduce all
passenger cars to a single type, called the "German car," with sixteen sizes and body designs.
They also expected to reduce the "German truck"
sizes to three — one-ton, two-ton, and five-ton
models. Similar standardization was planned
throughout industry. It was proposed that each
year the government should hold competitions
for designs and models, and should arrange production contracts among various firms in each
industry, which specified quotas to each factory.
In other words, all German automobile factories
would make the same sized parts. The number of
units each plant made would be arranged by the
government. The Nazis hoped by this standardization to reduce costs in industry and trade. It is
clear that they would have great advantages in

the export field by concentrating on a single model and by reducing the number of dealers now handling diverse lines.

5. *Racial Superiority*

[The central tenet of Nazi ideology is its racial theory. This has been somewhat misunderstood in the United States. We have been inclined to pay particular attention to the anti-Jewish measures of the Berlin government and its desire to Aryanize Germany. This anti-Semitic campaign is but a part of Nazi racial practice, which has, in the long run, a more ambitious program. Nazi racialism goes back to Wagner's mythology, to the myth of a superior Nordic race as propagated by the Frenchman, Gobineau, and the Englishman, H. S. Chamberlain.]The Nazis have brought forth a host of racial experts; probably the high priest could be identified as Professor Günther, now of the University of Berlin, the most prolific writer on the new theory, which is taught in German schools and universities, propagated in the press, radio, and public meetings, as well as worked out in practice.

23

The new racial theorists claim that the Nordic German race, with its original habitat on the shore of the Baltic, was the sole originator of culture and civilization. Its chief task must be to maintain its racial purity and prevent contamination with lesser tribes, some of whom may be all very well in their place, as carriers or transmitters of culture, but never its originators. Besides the Slavic and other races who have a legitimate future when devoting their energies to simple tasks such as agriculture, there is the single destructive Jewish race, which tears down culture and must therefore be exterminated. Racial theorists such as Staemmler assert that selective breeding can improve the German people and restore it to its original Nordic purity. He suggests that children who fail to pass twice in school might be sterilized. Hitler's elite body-guard, the S. S., is to be an example of new racial improvement. Only blond, blue-eyed Nordics may apply. Their prospective brides must submit to exacting physical measurements, for they cannot be more than so many inches shorter than their husbands, nor can their cheekbones and skulls show Slavic characteristics. Similarly, the points of their lower ear tips must be below the base of the nose, otherwise a taint of Semitic blood is indicated.⟩

I know of an S. S. doctor who compelled his family to have blood tests made for purposes of racial identification, but I never could find out what such tests are supposed to indicate. Günther points out that children of racially mixed marriages, for instance the offspring of a Swede and Belgian, will inherit two sets of physical and mental characteristics which will not match. The unfortunate child is doomed to be somewhat lopsided in body and mind. From the father's side he may inherit a large, vigorous pair of lungs, but from the mother such a weak heart that it will be unable to pump blood to the lungs, so that the child will have a tendency toward tuberculosis. Or the child may inherit from one parent a large and vigorous imagination, but from the other side of the family such a weak memory that it cannot remember what it imagines. This unfortunate state of affairs leads, in the view of the Nazis, to physical and mental maladjustments.

Bernhard Rust, the Prussian Minister of Culture, once explained in a nation-wide radio broadcast that Palestine was the crossroads of the ancient world. That here the black race of Africa, the white race of Europe, and the yellow race of Asia met and mingled to form a mongrel folk, the Jews. This gave the entire Jewish nation a sense of maladjustment, arising from their racial impurity. To explain this racial maladjustment, the Jewish religion with its conception of original sin was developed. But the maladjustment still persisted. Finally, in order to escape it, a new method of relief was proposed — the Messiah, later identified with Jesus Christ, who could save the soul from sin and thus restore the proper balance of mind and spirit.

Alfred Rosenberg, in his book *The Myth of the Twentieth Century*, explained that a pure race like the Nordic Germans have no maladjustment and no sense of sin. For them Christ becomes not only superfluous, but a degenerative influence. In other words, right and wrong are functions of race. If you belong to the proper race, whatever you do is automatically right. This is not to say that the average adult Nazi is fully convinced of this reasoning. Such revelations have not made wide headway among the older people of Germany, but are preached constantly to the German youth and the S. S., who will soon be the leaders of the state. For them the Nordic Germans exemplify a master race, divinely ordained to rule and lead lesser people. Only the blind, ignorant, and stubborn opposition of the inferior strains and the generous tolerance of the easygoing Germans have prevented the natural leaders of mankind from entering upon their historical mission. This delay has meant a fearful cost to humanity up to the present time. Hitler has come to lead his German people into their appointed place. Germany is the mother of culture; even Chinese art and literature sprang from Nordic wanderers who reached Asia distant years ago. The brilliance of Greece and Rome in classical times is explained by their beneficent infusion of Nordic blood, which was later polluted by racial admixtures, leading to the inevitable catastrophe. It is not only the Germans' right but their duty to assert their priority of blood to prevent the modern disintegration of human society, which started with the French Revolution and the Declaration of Independence, and to restore mankind to an ordered culture and civilization.

We must not overlook this thrilling message of racial superiority in Hitler's world scheme. No

German who has once listened to it can be quite the same again. Few of us are so hardheaded as not to have a feeling of elation and superiority when told that our blood is the most precious thing in the world, that merely by being alive we confer an inestimable blessing upon the earth, and that we have the divine right to leadership with the power and perquisites appertaining thereto. To poor, discouraged, hungry, and unemployed young Germans this doctrine appeared like a divine revelation. It explained the gulf between their inner pride and self-esteem and the wretched outward circumstances of their physical environment. It called for immediate, sustained, and determined action. All people of German descent or partial descent anywhere in the world tend to share these emotions. How could it be otherwise?

The weakness of this doctrine lies in its narrow appeal. How any Frenchman, Czech, or Dane could look forward with much happiness or assurance to a career of hewing wood and drawing water for German masters is hard to see. When Napoleon conquered Europe, he brought with him the spirit of the Revolution — the great ideals of liberty, equality, fraternity. These bore a message even to the conquered. But Hitler's philosophy promises nothing to the conquered but slavery and more slavery. Of course, the Nazi racial theory can be amended. Foreign racial groups have sometimes been described as *art-verwandt,* that is to say, similar in character to the Germans. For them may be reserved tolerable although subordinate stations in the coming world order. For the main body of Americans, however, there would seem to be little hope. Our blood has been so carelessly polluted by indiscriminate mixtures from all over Europe, not to speak of other parts of the world, that we are nothing but a degenerate mob. Some Nazis hold out the hope that the German strain in this country, which they sometimes claim to be fifteen or twenty million strong, may provide leadership and regeneration. Others, like the writer of romances, Hans Dominick, picture the German-Americans shaking the dust of this country from their feet and being colonized in Siberia, comparatively unpolluted after their period of alien bondage.

None of these prophecies seem to ring true. The German-Americans have been the most disappointing of all Germanic groups to the Nazis.

They have expressed irritating satisfaction with their present home and somehow seem to have dropped the inner urge to excel and conquer, which true Germans must exhibit. This quality of the German soul is, according to Hitler, the true mark of a real Nordic German; he cannot be identified by purely external characteristics. Such a revelation must be a satisfaction to Goebbels, Dr. Ley, and the Fuehrer himself. They look anything but Teutonic.

6. Economic Sterility

A feature of the National Socialist organization which makes it difficult to oppose is the parallel structure from top to bottom of both the State and the Party. These two organizations run down from the Fuehrer to the farthest corners of the Reich. Almost every government official is paralleled by an unofficial party functionary who has no government job but is perhaps just as powerful. In dealings with the outside . world the Nazis can alternatively use either the official mechanism or their party structure. For example, they may make a bargain with some foreign government regarding reciprocal use of each other's products, but the Nazi Party may order all loyal Germans to abstain from the use of the goods which the German government has formally allowed to be purchased. This nullifies the apparent concession. Such cases have been of frequent occurrence. The Nazis probably learned this trick from the parallel organizations of the Soviet government and the Third International in Russia.

The dual method of operation is particularly effective in evading the laws and regulations of foreign countries. What the German Embassies or Consulates are not allowed to do, they can have done by party representatives. For example, in the United States the German-American Bund is supposed to be an organization of American citizens; and no German citizens, let alone Germany's official representatives, are supposed to have anything to do with it, but it is in close touch with the National Socialist Party organization through unofficial channels.

One fundamental characteristic of all totalitarian economies is their essential unproductiveness. This arises first of all from their militaristic nature. They are economies of conflict, working toward an expansion of their territory and an increase in their power. They can never be disassociated from the thought of war. Hitler's solution of the employment problem is the stimulation of war industries. This is natural on psychological grounds because Nazi economy is an economy of conflict, and on material grounds because it seems easier for central planning to operate on militaristic than on peacetime methods. Peacetime production is too complex to lend itself to central planning, depending upon the whims of the ultimate consumer, but war production is uniform and standardized. It can be plotted in advance.

Authoritarian regimes tend to expand their bureaucracy. The number of uniforms constantly grows: in the armed forces of the land, sea, and air; in the ever-present police, of whom Germany has seven varieties — four kinds of Secret Police and three kinds of ordinary police. There is a growing body of party functionaries running all the way down to the block leader, responsible for the party loyalty and daily activities of a single block in each town and village. Membership in either National Socialist, Communist, or Fascist Party comes to be almost a

full-time job. There are so many forms to fill
out, so many committees to serve on, so many
meetings to organize, so much spying and snoop-
ing to do, that party members must in practice be
supported by the rest of the population. All this
leads to a topheavy economy, with not enough
primary producers. Some slack can be taken up
at the beginning as long as a certain amount of
unemployment remains over from a capitalist
economy; but when this has been ended through
increased war production, the economy from
then on tends to become more and more un-
productive.

In Germany the Nazis have been kept going
in the past through exploiting the Jews, the
Catholics, and other minority groups, cutting
down their property and income; by heavy taxa-
tion of wealthy citizens; by high-speed exploitation of mines and timber resources and intensive
exploitation of agriculture; by the nonpayment
of existing debts to foreigners and then the crea-
tion of more foreign indebtedness both monetary
and commodity; by the gradual consuming of
all liquid capital in the country; by exchanging
government short-term debt for existing securities held by private persons — then the bleeding

of the financial structure, including banks, insurance companies, trading houses, and manufacturing concerns, forcing them to exchange their equities for worthless government paper; and finally, when this process has gone on to its final limits, by preying upon other economies. Totalitarianism is by nature parasitic and predatory. It cannot live on its own resources, but must forever consume the wealth of its neighbors. The whole technique of German commercial policy is one of exploiting the assets of others. While the Nazi state grows ever more powerful, its citizens suffer continual reductions in their living standards. All totalitarian regimes must keep their peoples warlike and poor in order to hold them in line.

This essential sterility of the Fascist system is one explanation of its aggressiveness. The totalitarians are a group of bandits who have learned no useful trade or occupation but are well armed and have no scruples about attacking their neighbors. Germany has, under Hitler, thrown away her possibilities of peaceful trade and understanding with all the world and has no option but to go forward in the campaign of aggression. She must not, in Hitler's words, "export or die"; she must fight or die. Under these circumstances it is completely useless to await any peaceful settlement of Europe's troubles. The Nazis are not organized for peace. They are not prepared for it. They would not know what to do with it. I am convinced that if the German people were told that their period of war was over, that they could now look forward to a long, uninterrupted reign of peace, almost everyone would commence to think about his own private affairs and wonder, "Just what do I get out of all this?" Hitler must prevent things from ever settling down in this fashion. He must continually create emergencies to retain his control. The totalitarian state that has reached its objectives will blow up from internal pressure. For this reason there is no limit to be set upon Hitler's aggression. He dare not demobilize his armies or end his war economy. He has promised future wars to boys too young to participate in the present struggle. He has written in *Mein Kampf*, "The human race has grown great in war. In peace it would only decay." Dr. Ley, head of the Labor Front, in an especially characteristic outburst, declared in 1938, "In five years the German woman, her rifle in her hand, will bear her children in the trenches." At that time Europe was at peace. But it probably was the last peace any of us will ever see until totalitarianism is destroyed.

7. Falsehood and Treaty Breaking

The final aspect of National Socialist mentality which profoundly affects dealings with the outside world is an open and cynical disregard of truth and justice in carrying on negotiations either in war or in peace. Hitler has stated that "truth is anything which will help the German cause" and so, of course, changes from day to day. He has also stated that he is willing to make treaties and agreements from time to time, but, of course, anybody who believes in them is nothing more than a fool.

One day before our commercial treaty with Germany, containing a promise of equal treatment, had expired, I visited the Foreign Office to protest against the unfair discrimination practised upon our exporters of United States lard. The Foreign Office official explained at length that no discrimination existed, and imports of American lard were treated precisely as those from any other country, that our country had received a quota of 40 per cent of its average sales to Germany for the last three years, and that every other country was treated the same. Upon this, the American official who accompanied me reached into his pocket and brought out a Danish agricultural magazine, which contained the text of a secret agreement by which Denmark had been receiving a quota of 65 per cent compared to 40 per cent given us. The German official appeared only slightly embarrassed. He reached into his desk and pulled out the German text of the identical treaty and explained that that was the way things were done nowadays.

I said, "Well, what can we do now?"

He said, "You can file a protest."

"Yes, but we have already submitted a great number of protests, many of which have not even been answered and none of which appeared to do any good."

I took my hat and started for the door. The official accompanied me to the door and said, "I hope this little incident will not disturb our friendly personal relations, because I want you to remember that I have to earn my living somewhere." This was the only answer which the high official of the German government could give when his government had been caught in a flat lie and when their signature on our commercial treaty had been flagrantly and openly dishonored. I felt that there was little use of making further protests, and that there was less use of drawing up fresh treaties or agreements with people who dishonor their existing agreements so cynically. Honest old-fashioned Germans feel humiliated when they have to do Hitler's dirty work, but they do not seem able to make an effective stand for their principles. In Germany now only Hitler's opinion counts.

The long campaign for tearing up Germany's signature to the Treaty of Versailles and the propaganda which attempted to maintain that debts to foreigners should not be paid, if such payment would lower the German standard of living, bear bitter fruit. Now international respect for the sanctity of treaties is at a minimum. It is significant to note that no peace treaty closed the recent wars of Italy in Abyssinia or

Albania, that no peace has been signed in China, there was no peace treaty at the closing of the Spanish Civil War, and finally that Germany has signed no peace treaty with her conquered neighbors. It does not seem likely that the present European war, if Germany wins, will end in any treaty. There will be no peace conference, but simply the surrender of the conquered peoples on the basis of the best terms they can get individually.

One of the most disconcerting aspects of Hitler's tactics is that no one can find out his final terms. All nations or groups who have made agreements with the Nazis up to the present have found that these simply lead to the making of new agreements on harsher terms, that there is no final limit to what Hitler may demand from his victims. The people in conquered France, the Low Countries, Scandinavia, Poland, and Czechoslovakia live under suspense — their present situation is bad enough, and the future promises to be even worse. They cannot achieve any permanent place in the Nazi system, because whatever visible rights they now possess may be taken away from them at any moment. They have no possibility of reconstructing their shattered affairs on any permanent basis. They can only live and suffer from day to day. There seems no doubt that these tactics are well designed to lower the morale of the subjugated peoples and make them more pliable and helpless victims of the conqueror.

CHAPTER II

NAZI PLANS FOR WORLD EXPANSION

1. African Colonial Empire

THE preceding discussion of Nazi aims and ideas allows us to understand their basic policies. Now we shall consider the channels through which they operate and their plans for a future world. Among these plans perhaps the oldest is the campaign to restore Germany's prewar colonial empire in Africa, but on a scale larger than before and more intensively developed.

German plans for the continent of Africa largely fall within the sphere of activities of the German Colonial Society. This organization was reconstructed after the war from what was left of the colonial activities of the Second Reich. Until recently, General Von Lettow-Vorbeck, former Commander in Chief of East Africa, was the titular head. He was succeeded by General Ritter von Epp, Vice-Governor of Bavaria. The active head of the Colonial Society — as far as economic preparations go — has been in recent years Director Weigelt of the Deutsche Bank.

Most support comes from upper-class circles in Germany and from large industrial, commercial, and banking establishments. There has been little political activity so far, little interest aroused in National Socialist circles, and the whole movement seems to remain somewhat outside the realm of party doctrine and direction. This is probably because German aims in Africa are primarily economic ones.

The colonial plans do not envisage a large number of German emigrants to Africa, and there is little interest in the problems of government, education, and cultural activities. Africa is to remain the home of inferior colored peoples, who are to be put to work for the German state. It is believed that these people can be controlled and managed by a fairly small group of German officials, backed by only limited concentrations of the army and navy. The Germans believe that British success in governing India with only a small white army can be duplicated and surpassed in Africa.

I have never heard anyone in Germany discuss the welfare of the African natives or any plans for their future, except as coolies in the new commercial machine. The Nazis believe that

Germany possesses a reservoir of scientific knowledge, a wealth of useful energy, and powerful initiative and enterprise, which will, when transported to Africa, quickly reshape that continent into a vast reservoir of raw materials and food products needed in Europe. Africa is to contribute from her fields, forests, and mines. The Nazis are contemptuous of the slack, easygoing colonial methods of other powers. They refer to the fact that they have colonists but no colonies, while other nations have colonies but no colonists. They remind the world that sleeping sickness, long a scourge in British, Portuguese, Belgian, and French possessions, has only yielded to the discovery of *Germanin,* first synthesized by the I. G. Farben Industrie.

The Colonial Society has been conducting trials and experiments in new uses for African products. Years of research have been given to tropic woods such as balsa and okape. The society already knows just what trees are to be cut down and destroyed in the tropical forests and which ones will be cultivated and utilized. It is pointed out that in the hot climate of Central Africa large trees can mature in only seven years, and that it is foolish to procure lumber from Europe when Africa can be used as a cheaper and speedier source of supply. Plans have been made for the selective improvement of trees, shrubs, grasses, and many other plants which can successfully be grown there.

The society has detailed and far-reaching schemes of development which have not been made public, but some of which I learned from private conversations with their official representatives. For example, it is not planned to grow coffee in Africa, because Brazil has plenty of coffee for sale; and the pressure of the European market will be utilized to swing Brazil into the Nazi line-up. On the other hand, it is planned to expand the African production of rubber, quinine, cocoa, and a wide variety of tropical products. One particular industry which was already making considerable progress before the war was the cultivation and transportation of bananas from the West Coast to German ports. Most of the plantations lay in the Cameroons, a former Germany colony, now shared by the French and British. German companies were allowed to return there several years ago; narrow-gauge railroads were built to connect plantations with the ports; and the Woermann Line of steamships carried the product to Hamburg, where it began to displace Central American and West Indian fruit several years before the war. As an illustration of the extent to which colonial plans have been under way for many years, let me quote an experience of a Tacoma, Washington, lumberman who toured Germany, investigating methods of forestry and lumbering. During part of his trip, he was chaperoned by an extremely well-informed German forestry expert, who happened to mention that he had just recently resigned his position as head of the forestry of a native state in India. My friend wondered at this and asked him what had induced him to return to Germany. He stated that he had been appointed Chief Forester of the Cameroons.

"That is interesting. Have you any other foresters working with you?"

"Oh, yes, sixty at the present time."

"What are they doing?"

"Some of them are attending a foresters' school in East Prussia, and others are stationed throughout Germany, getting practical training."

This was several years before the war. Even at that time the Germans had gone so far with their plans that they had definitely appointed a number of the officials for the new African colonial state which they had not yet been able to conquer.

Director Weigelt explained to me at one time that his organization had been attempting for a long time to secure co-operation from the colonial offices of the British, French, and Dutch in the selection and improvement of new types of plants suitable for Africa. He cited the German effort to improve the present variety of the hevea, or most satisfactory rubber tree now grown in the Far East, and was very angry at the unwillingness of other countries to co-operate in these scientific developments. I well remember his saying that the time would come when Western nations would bitterly regret their slowness in allowing Germany to re-enter African colonization. He complained that years before the war the British, Portuguese, and French refused to allow rubber trees to be sent to Germany for experimental purposes. After all, one can hardly blame these other nations for not being enthusiastic about entering into German plans for conquering and exploiting their own territories.

There seems to be no doubt that the Nazis are correct in many of their beliefs and claims about

Africa. They could undoubtedly attack the problems of that Dark Continent with great resourcefulness and skill. One cannot, however, help but wonder what would be the fate of any unfortunate natives who might fail to adjust themselves to German plans. They would get the surprise of their lives, but they probably would not live long. In fairness to the Germans, it might be said that most African natives would probably fit in very well with the proposed scheme. They might consider the addition of a swastika armband an attractive touch of color to their scanty costumes, and a Fascist salute and "Heil Hitler" greeting could be easily learned.

No doubt, under the Nazi rule the natives would have to work very hard. They would be given low pay and strictest discipline. But they would also have the benefit of the best medical attention, scientific hospital treatment, and prisons operated upon modern and efficient lines. They would be compelled to clean up their filthy huts, disinfect their villages, install modern roads and communications. Africa would be one great German slave plantation operated on scientific lines and thriving on low-cost production of tropic staples for export. Whatever products competitive with our own could be grown there would quickly oust American goods from other markets. Cotton, of course, is an outstanding example of such a commodity.

2. *German Citizens Abroad*

Quite different is the Nazi drive upon German citizens abroad. These *Reichs-Deutsche* are persons still possessing German citizenship and, for the most part, born in the home country. They are directly under the control of a special section of the German Foreign Office and come under Gauleiter Bohle, in a separate *Gau* or province of the Reich. Their names are card-indexed and classified in Berlin. Every one of them is supposed to be a missionary of *Deutschtum* in the foreign world. They are supposed to be ready to return to the fatherland if summoned and be at all times available for such duties as may be assigned to them. The most reliable of these Germans abroad are, of course, the members of the National Socialist Party and its subordinate organizations. But not many possess the coveted membership card. Outside the pale are the émigrés and well-known non-Nazis, who have boldly offended the organization. In the middle lie the majority. Many of them left Germany for peace of mind or other reasons of their own; and while they do not desire to offend the powers-that-be in their own country, they also have their lives to live and their living to earn in the lands where they are domiciled. Their plight is a dangerous one, as they are under pressure from two sides at once and are always more or less under suspicion, no matter what side they really take.

To illustrate this: it has been a favorite custom of the Nazi agents abroad to circularize German citizens with a plea that any anti-Nazi propaganda be promptly reported to the nearest German Consulate. At the same time, the Nazis themselves send anti-Nazi literature to their mailing list of German citizens and check off which ones turn it in. All the rest can be labeled as dangerous anti-Nazis. This sort of thing has been going on all over the world.

I recently received a letter from a young German in Guatemala who says that he might just as well have never left Germany as far as getting away from the Nazis is concerned — that it is

dangerous to say a word against Hitler on the
coffee plantation where he works or in the surrounding country, which is full of German
planters, and that he is afraid he might be kid-
naped aboard a German ship and taken back
home to serve his time in the army. Incidentally,
he wrote that his plantation had sold its 1940
coffee crop to Germany against the delivery of
German merchandise from Hamburg as soon
as the British blockade should be broken, which
was soon expected. That coffee may have to keep
a long time.

At the head of the organization of Germans
abroad stands Gauleiter Bohle, who is now considered the second most important man in the
German Foreign Office. Ever since Neurath was
replaced by Ribbentrop, the Bohle organization
has increased in strength and influence. In contrast to the other departments of the Foreign
Office with their suave and polite officials, reminiscent of the old regime, the *Auslands Abtei-
lung* is staffed with young, aggressive Nazis
who are somewhat contemptuous of their more
correct, moth-eaten colleagues. The old eight-
eenth-century buildings at Nos. 74, 75, and 76
Wilhelmstrasse that house the Foreign Office re-

mind the visitor of past epochs in Germany's history. The general architectural plan has a strong flavor of early Prussian severity enveloped by the nationalism of Frederick the Great and the rococo gaiety of the Napoleonic period. Here in austere simplicity stand the apartments of Bismarck; here Hindenburg spent the years of his presidency. The atmosphere is full of German history, but none of it seems to be in accord with the present regime. It is very hard to imagine the Great Elector or the Iron Chancellor looking with pleasure upon these their successors.

A few years back a young German in Nazi uniform came in to see me with a story that he had been decoyed back to Germany under false pretenses. He had been living in the Pacific Coast states, but had never become an American citizen. At the request of a relative, he had returned to Germany to work in the propaganda service of the National Socialist Party. He told me that he had been greatly disappointed, that his dreams of a grand and better Reich were destroyed, and that there was nothing he wanted more than to get out of the country and go back to the United States and become an American citizen. In checking up on his story, I asked him the name of

his relative who had induced him to enter the
party service. He said, "Why, his name is Bohle,
and he has an important position in the Foreign
Office."

3. *Racial Germans*

Stuttgart, the metropolis of Southwestern
Germany, has for years been the home of the
V.D.A., or Association of Germans Abroad. This
organization is older than its counterpart in the
Foreign Office, but only achieved international
notoriety after the rise of the Nazi Party. Its
unique field is the organization of the *Volks-
Deutsche*, or "racial Germans," all over the
world. These people are all members of the great
German *Volk*. Their citizenship lies in their
blood, and their passport is a common cultural
inheritance; their number is legion — perhaps
thirty, forty, or fifty million. Awkwardly enough
for the Nazis, however, every one of these racial
Germans is a citizen of some foreign country.
That is the distinguishing mark which sets them
apart from the *Reichs-Deutsche* or "German
citizens."

According to the stupid and unnatural laws of foreign countries, these racial Germans are supposed to owe allegiance to the country in which they reside, own property, and maintain their citizenship. Included in this group are an indefinite number of German-Americans in the United States, estimated at from fifteen to twenty-five million persons; about three million more in Latin America; numbers of Volga Germans in the Soviet Union; German racial islands in Rumania, Yugoslavia, Hungary, and other areas; German colonists in mandated territories. An even larger group is comprised of those racial Germans in the area which separated before or during the Peace of Westphalia in 1648 and which has not yet been gathered back to the bosom of Mother Germania. Such obstinate groups are a majority of the Swiss, the Dutch, the Flemish, the Alsatians, and part of the Danes. Formerly included in the group were German minorities in areas which have now been incorporated in the Reich — Austrians, Sudeten Germans, and the Germans in Poland. There are even a considerable number of racial Germans in Canada, Australia, South Africa, Italy, and other places. In fact, it is difficult to think of any spot where there are not some representatives of this group.

Obviously the political ties which connect such persons with the fatherland must either be extremely tenuous or be maintained underground. The best method of fostering the loyalty and co-operation of such groups is by channels which are apparently nonpolitical. It is good strategy to emphasize language, culture, education, literature, science, sports, music, and other more or less harmless media. Every summer an annual get-together is held in Stuttgart for racial Germans from all over the world. It should be a source of considerable comfort to Americans to know that the V.D.A. considers the German-American group, although perhaps the largest in point of numbers, to be the most unsatisfactory of all. The German-Americans have shown less enthusiasm, less obedience, and put up smaller contributions per capita than any of the others.

This interesting fact probably has its origin in history. Many of the Germans who came to the United States were not representative of their nation as a whole. Particularly around 1848 occurred an important emigration of German liberals and democrats to the United States as a result of the failure of the liberal revolution in that year. These people, of the type of Carl Schurz, came to join the American democracy and deliberately cut political allegiances of the past. Before and since that particular wave of political refugees, large numbers of German emigrants came to this country for economic reasons. For the most part they came from South and West Germany, the areas most affected by Western Christian civilization for two thousand years. They were largely composed of small farmers and artisans. They had never been subjected to the rigidity of Hohenzollern rule and for the most part remained untouched by the blood-and-iron philosophy of Bismarck, the intense nationalism of Fichte, and did not acquire the stern traits which matured in the Germans of the Northeast in their thousand-year struggle with the Slavs.

Such German emigrants brought with them the domestic German culture of the village — the church and the *Vereine*. But they did not bring the modern super-Germanism of the universities and the national patriotic societies, such as the Colonial Society and the Navy League. They were mostly in moderate circumstances, came in at the bottom of the economic structure, worked hard to get their foothold on the ladder of success in the new world, and gladly assimilated the political, economic, and cultural background of their new home. The German-Americans became Americans, with only a pleasant and harmless German flavor to give a reminder of their origin.

Quite different were the circumstances of emigration of other German racial groups in Latin America, the tropical countries, and certain parts of Central Europe. Many of these people had been colonized in a body, bringing their own leaders with them, bringing their pastors, schoolteachers, newspapers, and their own integrated industrial and agricultural systems. They settled in compact groups among peoples who were economically inferior and supposedly of a lower cultural status. The Germans in Brazil, Rumania, and the Volga region had little incentive to adopt the manners and customs of the surrounding natives. Their own institutions were probably superior.

Even after years of separation from the homeland, they have maintained their individuality as colonists and not as mere citizens of their new home. In South America, German schools are often the best schools, the German pastors the most able and successful, the German newspapers, athletic and social clubs, the leading institutions of the locality. Such racial groups were often strengthened by the later arrival of Germans of particular training and ability: wealthy men who purchased plantations, built factories, established importing and exporting concerns, shipping lines, and other undertakings; German officers who arrived to train local armed forces; German engineers who built bridges and electric power plants. In this way the Germans of Brazil or Rumania have remained much more German than those who came to the United States and can be counted upon as more effective and reliable supporters of the V.D.A.

In other words, the Germans who came to the United States were mostly poor and brought only a certain segment of Germanism with them. They started in at the bottom and worked up, partly in imitating their American neighbors. The Germans who went to other countries moved in at the top. They brought the whole of Germanism with them and have largely retained it.

Since these racial Germans are all citizens of foreign countries and since their German citizenship is one of blood only and not of the law courts, official German organizations can work with them only at the risk of international complications. For this reason, it has appeared more feasible to knit such groups together by unofficial organizations, affiliated not with the German government, but with the National Socialist Party and its network of subsidiary organizations. In particular the following organizations have been prominent in the support of the V.D.A. program: the S. A. or Storm Troopers, the S. S. or Elite Guard, the Hitler Youth for work among boys, the *Deutsche Maedel* or organization of German girls, the *Frauenschaft* or National Socialist women's organization. Most of these groups have organized comparable associations in foreign countries. In the United States the most prominent of these in the public eye has been the Bund, which is the American equivalent to the Storm Troopers. Less prominent among these organizations are the German-American Alliance and a host of minor societies for all sorts of purposes and covering every age, sex, and occupational group. The general purpose of these societies is to maintain and foster cultural and racial ties with the homeland, to raise funds for National Socialist purposes, and whenever possible to lay the foundation for political and military co-operation with the Nazi regime and the incorporation of the particular foreign country in a German world pattern.

Among the functions of the Minister of Propaganda is the control of German advertising by means of a body called the Advertising Council. This concern has urged all persons of German blood abroad, whether citizens of the Reich or not, to show their loyalty by purchasing at least four dollars' worth of German goods per month. They are also urged to go to their local merchants and demand particular German trade-marked goods, with the idea that in this way such goods can be widely introduced everywhere. The German abroad is supposed to be an active missionary for his fatherland's goods and culture by using German drugs and medicines, subscribing to German newspapers and periodicals, tuning his German radio to one of the directional beams from the fatherland every day, and incidentally making regular contributions both to the National Socialist Party at home and to its local organization in the country where he happens to reside. The amount of money which has been taken out of the United States in this way is tremendous. In such a manner the propaganda organization abroad can help to finance itself.

It can also be financed by the judicious use of pressure upon Germany's enemies. For example, I knew the case of a Jew who had a small factory in Vienna, making ladies' handbags. He had a branch establishment in Brussels. When the Nazis took over Austria, this Jew was placed in a concentration camp until he had handed over his Austrian property. He was then allowed to leave the country, and fled to his branch in Brussels. After about a month's respite, two Nazis approached him to say that his brother who remained in Austria was now arrested and in a concentration camp, but the brother would be allowed to leave Austria if he would put up $5,000 each for the two Nazis and $10,000 as a contribution to the National Socialist Party work in Argentina. The poor fellow was so sorry for his brother that he did this. Of course now the Nazis have taken over Belgium and have him again in their power.

62

4. High Pressure through Exchange Control

Perhaps the most far-reaching channel for the Nazi movement to reach and influence the rest of the world has been the ordinary business and commercial contact between Germany and other countries. Before Hitler came to power in 1933, Germany had already taken a number of steps to centralize foreign trade and financial control in the hands of the central government. The principal device used was the control of all foreign trade transactions and a maze of departmental regulations. Exchange control has long been a method of protecting a threatened currency from extreme depression and from the attacks of international bear speculators. When exchange control was introduced in Germany in July 1931, it was considered an emergency measure to stop the drain on Germany's gold and foreign exchange reserves and to bring the nation's balance of trade and balance of payments into proper alignment. Only after the re-emergence of Dr. Schacht in the Reichsbank during the spring of 1933 did it appear evident that the Nazis had made a virtue of necessity and were using the totalitarian control of foreign commerce transactions as an offensive as well as a defensive weapon.

Foreign exchange control sets up a wall around the country at the frontier and insures that no currency, negotiable instruments, or other securities can pass that frontier without a special permit from the authorities. As a corollary to this control, a censorship of mails must be installed to prevent leakages. Travelers must be searched in the ports and telegram and cablegram money transfers placed under censorship. After a short experience of exchange control, it appeared that to make it effective control must also be extended over the movement of commodities to prevent possible emigrants from putting their domestic funds into goods, shipping those goods across the frontier, reselling them abroad in foreign currency, and decamping with the proceeds. Money control, to be effective, must be extended over movements of goods.

Shortly after the Nazis came in they ruled that when German exports were paid for by the foreign customer the payment in foreign exchange must be deposited with the Reichsbank within three days of its receipt. Imports of commodities were at first controlled by allotting established import houses a monthly quota of foreign exchange, expressed as a percentage of their former average import needs. This quota, which started at 80 per cent of former imports, fell to 10 per cent by the summer of 1934, at which time exchange rationing was placed on a day-to-day basis. On September 24, 1934, Dr. Schacht's new plan was put into operation; this stopped all possibility of imports, except under specific permit from the government.

Twenty-five import-control offices, allocated according to commodities, administered the new regulations and allowed permits for the importation of necessities. By 1935 necessities were defined as goods of military significance. In the beginning, the control offices attempted to apply rough-and-ready methods for rationing imported commodities as best they could. It proved rather difficult to put the economic life of a great people in a strait jacket so quickly, but the German people responded by restricting their consumption of foreign goods; and the new system got under way without too much friction or difficulty.

I called upon most of the control offices within a few days of their establishment and found that it was impossible to see the officials. There had been so many applications from business men that it was necessary to bar the doors and handle only written communications. I could not even get in touch with the officials by telephone. In the case of the office handling food products, the number of employees increased from twelve or fifteen at the start to twelve hundred at the end of two weeks. It proved necessary to engage a Berlin theater in order to handle interviews with importers. The officials and staff appeared upon the stage, while the importers were allowed to enter the main body of the theater. Then one commodity after another was taken up. One official would call, "The next item is tomatoes. All dealers interested in tomatoes come to the front." Perspiring produce handlers bolted up toward the stage and a short session ensued. Each one then would tell his story: "I have two carloads of tomatoes on the Dutch frontier. They are rotting because we cannot get an import license.". . . "I have two hundred boxes of

66

tomatoes on order from Italy." . . . "I have a consignment of tomatoes due in Hamburg harbor and don't know what to do with them." And so on. After a while, by rule of thumb, a certain order was secured, and a rough-and-ready allocation of exchange made for the tomato situation. The same thing occurred in the case of onions, potatoes, lettuce, and all other perishable commodities. In a more leisurely way, this control was extended over nonperishable goods until everything was on a permit basis.

Lawyers in Germany have very largely ceased to function as interpreters of the law, because, as I said earlier, courts are instructed to render decisions according to "healthy public opinion." A knowledge of the written law is no longer of such importance as before. This gave an opportunity to Germany's lawyers to engage in the securing of permits. Since every transaction, foreign and later domestic, necessitated such documents, the legal profession quickly became permit procurers or fixers. The fast trains leading to Berlin from the provinces were labeled "permit trains," because they were principally occupied by legal gentlemen coming to government offices in search of these indispensable documents.

Large sums of money changed hands in the course of these operations. One lawyer in Berlin's west end told me that as a result of such negotiations he had now become the largest owner of properties in the cloak, suit, and clothing business of the country.

The foreign-trade permit system led to monopolies in the imported articles, and the monopolists were not slow to take advantage of their favorable situation by price increases. To counteract such tendencies, the government was forced to set up a price control governing imported commodities, and later on was forced to control the prices of goods made from imported raw materials. A logical extension of this system forced controlled prices throughout German economy.

As a necessary corollary of controlled prices, it was found expedient to allocate production among domestic firms. Production in both agriculture and industry was put upon a quota basis. Some time previously, wages had also been set at fixed levels by thirteen labor trustees, appointed by the government under the National Labor Law of 1934. Wages were in general set at the 1932 levels, with certain provisions for bonuses in defense industries. Finally, the control of wages and the control of production led in 1938 to the control of jobs.

Even before the present war started, German employees were frozen at their existing desks or workbenches. It was assumed that everyone was a soldier taking a part in the national effort and should not be allowed to seek other employment merely because it paid better or seemed more suitable. Young persons entering industry and agriculture are now assigned to their jobs by the government, and once entering them must continue. A laborer cannot even plead illness and remain idle at home without producing a physician's certificate; while government inspectors have combed night clubs, bars, summer resorts, and winter-sport headquarters in search of sons of the idle rich for whom a job is waiting. Thus the introduction of control at the frontier has finally led to a complete control of wages, prices, and jobs throughout the German economy.

In the beginning, it was somewhat difficult to divine exactly what principles lay behind the allocation or refusal of permits. Government officials appeared to be so pressed by circumstances beyond their control that they were compelled

to follow the line of least resistance and act upon
a simple opportunist plan. Like Eliza crossing
the river by jumping from one cake of ice to
another, German government officials met each
situation by jumping from one emergency to
the next. In the hectic days of 1934, when the
old economic order was dying, Dr. Schacht
presided over the Reichsbank, assisted by four
younger stalwarts named Brinkmann, later on
Vice-President of the Reichsbank and Assistant
Secretary of Economics, destined to go insane
from overwork; Blessing, a director of the
Reichsbank; Wohlthat, now considered the
Reich's most able trade negotiator; and Herbert
Goering, a cousin of the fat and famous Hermann. These "four horsemen" alternated between the offices of Minister of Economics and
the Reichsbank. In their shirtsleeves, arguing in
loud voices reminiscent of General Hugh John-
son and the NRA, they plugged up the loopholes,
rationed commodities, pieced together the country's economic machine when it threatened to
break down entirely. Each day brought a succession of emergencies. In the morning, a shortage of copper might threaten the electrical industry with a sudden shutdown. By afternoon the

danger had shifted to lubricating oil or bauxite. Quick plans were made from day to day to import and ration just enough of the essential commodities to keep things going. These officials performed miracles of energy and improvisation.

5. Manipulation of Clearing Agreements

But a greater wonder was in store. Dr. Schacht and his colleagues slowly evolved a system by which Germany's economic difficulties were turned into advantages and a new type of economic pressure developed which has proved successful in most parts of the world since 1934. Whether this was by accident or design no one can say. To the Nazi economists goes the credit for working out a system of living on their debts. They realized the implications of the well-known fact that a dishonest debtor has all the advantage over his creditor and that international trading is not enforced by the sanction of any court.

The broad lines of Schacht's economic policy were, first, to segregate Germany's trade relations from participation in any international network of commercial and financial transactions, establishing a series of independent bilateral relations with individual foreign countries. Or in other words, Germany's foreign trade was no longer to be international trade but a system of parallel but separate relations with other states. When trade was thus sorted out, it became apparent that Germany's position vis-à-vis other countries varied from a creditor relationship in some areas, notably Eastern and Central Europe, to an aggravated debtor position toward the United States and most Latin American and Western European countries — and varied from an import balance of around eight hundred million marks with the United States to small export balances in other directions. This fact set the stage for the establishment of separate and differing regulations with each foreign country. The practice of barter had already taken hold among the countries of Eastern Europe, who were all desperately short of cash. Germany resolved it from an unrelated series of individual transactions to an organized national policy. Separate barter dealings were merged and a framework raised to clear all commodity movements between Germany and other states.

Such clearing agreements, frequently revised and amended, covered the bulk of German transactions. They were divided into state-arranged clearings, set up by foreign treaty arrangements between governments, and central bank-clearing agreements, regulated by the German Reichsbank on one side and central banks abroad on the other. Both types provided that as a rule no transactions were to be for cash but that exporters in Germany would ship, for example, to Yugoslavia and be credited with the mark value of their shipments by the German Reichsbank. Yugoslav exporters to Germany would be credited in dinars by the central bank in Belgrade, with the two banks balancing accounts. Payment was credited to the exporters in each country in their local currency, and at the end of the year the balance would be carried forward in favor of one or the other country to apply against next year's transactions. Theoretically, this type of national clearing was an acceptable method of conducting trade between bankrupt states, and was widely held as a device for increasing international trade, or at least maintaining it under difficult circumstances.

In practice, however, bilateral trade between

any pair of countries almost never results in an exact balance. One or the other country has an excess of exports. Its balance must be carried forward into the next year and certain exporters must wait for payment out of new import transactions. As a rule, the factors which have originally made for an unbalanced trade persist and will lead to greater one-sided balances in subsequent years. Some exporters in a country with an export balance have to wait for their money for a longer and longer period. Finally, there is pressure put upon trade circles in the exporting country to hold down shipments to equal or cut under current imports from the debtor country. If this proves successful, the other country retaliates by reducing its balance, both nations jockeying for position and each attempting to hold down its exports below its imports through fear of delays in payments and eventual losses.

It was not long before most of my commercial attaché colleagues in Berlin, whose countries were working under clearings, spent a great part of their efforts in preventing shipments from their own countries to Germany, since they were fearful of running up too big a credit and finally being forced to take a loss. The Minister from

Nicaragua in Berlin proudly explained that he had succeeded in stopping Nicaraguan shipments to Germany before they exceeded German goods sent to Nicaragua, and his government even went so far as to make sure that German goods entering Nicaraguan ports should actually be unloaded from the ships and placed in warehouses on the docks under Nicaraguan control before they allowed compensating products to be loaded. In this way, the little country managed to keep on the debtor side and could avoid the high-pressure tactics of the German debtor. Other countries were less cautious. They swallowed the German bait, hook and all, enthusiastically shipping commodities with little thought of how they were eventually to be paid.

The Germans on their part were bursting with optimism and big ideas. They were willing to negotiate for the entire crops of smaller countries at attractive prices, and blandly explained that of course they were not paying cash, but that the little country could certainly obtain from Germany in payment a wide variety of suitable articles well designed to meet its needs.

The small one-crop countries of Latin America and Eastern Europe proved to be easy meat for the Germans. Most of these nations had been suffering from the stagnation of world trade, and marketing of their main crops in an era of low prices was their principal economic headache. Now mighty Germany, a consuming unit of nearly 70,000,000 persons, appeared willing to buy the whole crop. All marketing problems were at an end. The pressure of producing groups upon the local governments bested any skeptical fears about the suitability or availability of German goods in exchange; furthermore, most of these producers' groups were better organized and more vigorous than the remaining mass of people. They knew what they wanted — quick sales at a high price, reimbursement out of the funds of their central bank; and they were perfectly willing to let their government hold the bag and collect from Germany as best it could.

As an example, the South African government, under pressure from domestic wool growers, sold its entire wool clip to Germany against the future delivery of German locomotives, automotive equipment, and similar commodities. Unfortunately, as time elapsed the South Africans were unable to get deliveries of German automobiles at prices which were at all in line with the cars offered from the United States and other countries. German locomotive plants seemed unable to deliver equipment which would suit the South African railroads, and the export of different types of electrical equipment, machinery, and tools was prohibited, as these products were needed for the German army; so when twelve months had elapsed, the wool sales still remained on the books, and little had been taken by South Africa in payment. Nevertheless, the second wool clip was marketed in the same way as the first; another year saw a third clip go the way of its predecessors. Germany had obtained its wool, woven it into uniforms for the army; and the South Africans were still whistling for suitable German products in payment.

In this way the German negotiators incurred a huge commodity indebtedness with the outside world. The Germans had done it again. First in the years 1919–1923 they had financed themselves by selling paper marks to foreigners, hot from the printing press. Then from 1924 to 1929 they kept going by selling long-term bonds through investment banking houses. As the world depression deepened, they obtained short-term bank advances; and now when their financial credit was completely exhausted, they borrowed commodities. Dr. Schacht had realized that an honest debtor worries about his obligations and desires to keep them at a minimum; a dishonest debtor lets his creditors do the worrying for him and tries to run up his obligations as high as possible, because he is not planning to pay anyhow.

The German Ministry of Economics then began to see other advantages to be derived from this system. The Nazis could get rid of unsalable stocks of merchandise on long-term credits to individual merchants in foreign countries. It was easy for them to extend credit to any foreign merchant in a country which operated a clearing because the local government was holding the bag, not the Germans. Another device was to use commodities obtained under the clearing for resale in cash markets. The price didn't particularly matter, because the goods were obtained on credit, sold for cash; the cash could be used for propaganda, the purchase of war materials, and other urgent needs, and the final bills would not be paid anyway until they were finally obliterated in the next war. In this way Germans resold Brazilian coffee, Bulgarian tobacco,

Greek currants, and obtained cash for airplane parts from the United States and Great Britain.

Naturally, such tactics began to upset the world market for the commodities of the unfortunate one-crop countries. They could only squirm and wriggle but could not escape from the new economy in which they were enmeshed. Instead of breaking off trade with Germany, their inability to sell in other markets made them more dependent upon their bulk customer. They were forced to sell an even larger proportion of their crop to Germany than before.

In this way the Nazi economists believed that Germany could make herself the world's middleman and that overseas buyers would have to come to Berlin for all sorts of foreign commodities. In fact, before the present war, American buyers of Oriental tobacco and similar products found that they could buy for cash in Berlin more cheaply than any place else in the world. In these negotiations, the Germans seemed quite unmindful of considerations which would ordinarily limit a commercial transaction. The representative of an American pack firm told me that he was shown in Hamburg two shiploads of Argentine beef, obtained by Germany on a credit basis at a price of fourpence a pound. The ships were never unloaded, but were redirected to Rotterdam, where the meat was sold to the Dutch for cash at two and one-half pence per pound, or a loss of three United States cents per pound. These funds were then used to purchase a large quantity of straw which the German army apparently needed quickly. For what purposes it is unknown.

One of the most disturbing factors of this clearing system was the special arbitrary values placed upon the German reichsmark for the purposes of the clearings. These values varied between countries and were arranged to suit particular circumstances. Sometimes the rate at which the exchange was to be computed was kept completely secret. This left foreign competitors entirely in the dark and was a most unsettling element in world business. The Germans developed an entire new system of multiple values for their currency and used them as a sharp-edged weapon for price cutting and subsidy. Aside from the separate and sometimes secret values for the mark specified in the agreements were the fluctuating values of the so-called *Aski* marks, which were varied according to countries. This necessitates a short explanation regarding blocked currency.

When foreign-exchange regulations came into force in 1931, German mark balances owned by foreigners inside Germany could not be freely exchanged for other currencies. The export of German currency notes was also prohibited. A foreigner with a mark balance in a German bank found his funds blocked. He could only obtain access to them under permit. Funds of this type were called simply "blocked marks." In case such funds had arisen from the sale of securities or real estate, they could only be invested inside Germany on long term — that is, for a minimum of five years. This type of blocked marks were called security marks and were soon discounted at a greater figure than the ordinary blocked variety. Marks owned by persons desiring to leave the country were blocked as emigrant marks. Marks held by foreign banks under the standstill agreement were available for resale at a discount to tourists and travelers entering Germany and were called travel marks. Finally, the mark balances arising from the sale of foreign commodities in Germany under the new arrangements or under special permits were blocked as *Aski* marks. Since these marks were only available for purchase of German goods, designed to be exported to the specific country of ownership of the funds, and since trade movements varied from country to country, these newly created *Aski* marks were discounted at varying rates, differing from each other, and the whole series of discounts fluctuating from day to day. To put it in another way, there were Brazilian *Aski* marks arising from the sale of Brazilian goods to Germany which differed in value from Rumanian *Askis* or United States *Askis*. Our particular variety was sharply discounted, owing to the overweight balance of trade from the United States to Germany; and these marks lost their value entirely in 1936 under a treasury anti-dumping ruling.

In addition to these types, there were a large number of special marks arising from individual agreements between foreign shippers and the German government. For example, John Smith, who had shipped palm oil to Germany from Africa, had a special mark of his own, with a special discount and special arrangements and restrictions upon its use. No foreign financiers were able to thread this jungle of multiple mark values with much success, especially since the German government made all the rules and changed them from day to day.

6. *Dumping and Subsidies*

The entry of a powerful totalitarian state, backed by the manifold resources of German industry, into world trade produced many upsets, usually with unfortunate consequences for international commercial relations. Nations which were either situated close to the German frontier or had a large part of their trade with the Reich were forced to adjust their own methods of doing business in order to fit it to the Nazi picture. It was necessary for them to maintain two sectors of their economy — one semi-controlled to work with the controlled economy of Germany, and the other relatively uncontrolled which maintained ordinary trade relations with the Western democratic powers. There is an innate tendency for measures of control to spread over a larger area, and the experience of the years before the recent war showed a constant tendency for the totalitarian trade methods to extend themselves into countries supposed to be operating on a free economy. Single firms are unable to buck a totalitarian machine. They called for help from their own governments and in this way a certain measure of totalitarian economic control was set up even in countries which professed to eschew such methods.

Furthermore, German commercial policy continually aimed at expanding its share of the world. Germans insisted that they needed more living space. This apparently means a larger area of land for German people to live in, as well as an increasing block of subsidiary states acting as markets and suppliers of raw materials. High-pressure methods were constantly at work to enlarge this area. To put it in simpler terms, the Germans, together with their Axis allies, would suddenly approach a small neighboring country, already closely enmeshed in totalitarian trade schemes, with a demand somewhat as follows: "The new order is now doing 60 per cent of your foreign business. We are your largest market and largest source of supply. You must choose whether to join us completely or lose every bit of this existing business." In practically every case these demands were successful. In this way smaller nations were steadily brought into the enlarged orbit of the totalitarians. The addition of each new nation created a greater economic block and enlarged the possibilities of pressure on the next neighboring states. This had the effect of gradually narrowing the area of free economy in the world, causing tremendous fluctuations in prices, rapid movements of commodities, and cable transfers of funds from one center to another. London, Paris, Amsterdam, and even New York, began to feel that their world was shrinking.

Totalitarian trade methods are political and military in purpose. Mere economic considerations carry no weight. It has been proved impossible to have pure business relations with the Nazis. For the Nazis it was not merely a case of "trade follows the flag." In their highly organized system, trade, military alignments, use of German officers for training, troops, the establishment of Nazi radio stations and newspaper chains, airlines, shipping, German schools, exchanges of students and professors, all marched together, each an element in the Nazi drive. Such a movement illustrates dramatically what is meant by the word *totalitarian*.

One of the most effective ways of extending German trade pressure on the outside world was the direct use of government subsidy. In addition to subsidies obtained by the use of multiple value currency, there was also the subsidy from repatriation of German dollar bonds in the United States, which were bought by German exporters and resold at a higher price at home.

Then there was a subsidy obtained by buying scrip, used to pay foreign bondholders in place of cash. The discount on the scrip was 50 per cent, but it of course vanished at the time of nonpayment of interest on German bonds. Finally there was a subsidy paid directly to exporters by the Gold Discount Bank. This was collected through a levy assessed upon German business enterprises by their own trade associations, and it was enforced in case of nonpayment by the government seizing property and selling it, just as in the case of any other tax. According to the last peacetime figures, the levy was running about one and a half billion marks per year, or roughly 40 per cent of German exports. This means that the average German export transaction obtained a 40 per cent subsidy from the German government at the expense of domestic industry. In particular cases, of course, the subsidy was much higher. Some years ago, when the average subsidy on all shipments was 25 per cent, a German coal exporter told me that he was getting a 65 per cent subsidy on coal shipped to South Africa. In other words, the South African customer paid only 35 per cent of the total price and the German government paid the remainder. Private American companies can never compete in price with commodities subsidized in this way by a totalitarian government, especially if that control is extended over the whole of the resources of Europe.

7. *Political Aims of Nazi Business Transactions*

A totalitarian Europe would operate its economy through highly organized, centralized control. We should not be able to negotiate agreements with individual firms over there. Everything would be routed through a government agency. This is an essential part of totalitarian economic practice. We should have to operate under the regulations laid down by dictators famous for insistence on their own way. The Nazis believe in 100 per cent or nothing — and 100 per cent for them and nothing for us would be the usual arrangement.

I well remember how American firms who completed business negotiations through the Nazi government up to last year were compelled to ship their goods on German ships, use German insurance companies, make a contract enforceable under German law and in German courts, provide at their own expense for German inspectors who came to this country in advance of shipments. The Nazis even insisted that contracts made with German firms should carry a printed clause to the effect that "this contract is made under National Socialist principles." No American knew what National Socialist principles were, and we were never able to find out in advance. In practice, however, this meant that the American firm was strictly bound to the contract but that the Germans were able to get out of it at any time by quoting such versions of National Socialist principles as they cared to apply at the moment.

We must get this straight once and for all: there is no such thing as having purely economic relations with the totalitarian states. Every business deal carries with it political, military, social, propaganda implications.

About three years ago Goebbels's Ministry of Propaganda arranged for the president of the German Film Chamber to visit my office to discuss an exchange of motion pictures. The Propaganda Ministry proposed that American companies bring their productions into Germany, sell pictures for what they could get, and take out their profit without restrictions. In return, Goebbels demanded the right to one quarter of the playing time of the largest picture theater in each of our twenty-five largest cities for pictures sent over by the Ministry of Propaganda. I found it impossible to convince the Propaganda Ministry that the United States government had no power to compel theater owners to display any particular pictures.

Some time after my experience in the film transaction, Dr. Goebbels approached another American official in Berlin with a proposal for a better understanding regarding newspaper publicity and radio broadcasting. He was pained by insults offered to the Fuehrer in the American press and radio broadcasts. To show his good

will he proposed to our Embassy that we select
some Nazi journalist or radio broadcaster whom
we disliked. As a friendly gesture, Dr. Goebbels
promised that he would arrest the offending
Nazi within twenty-four hours and give him
just the sort of punishment we suggested. "Now
why can't we have the same sort of friendly co-
operation on the part of the American government?" said he. Such incidents illustrate how
difficult it would be to come to an understanding
with the totalitarians.

Now this was before the war broke out, and
the Nazis thought they were treating us well.
We were really being given special consideration.
To imagine the sort of treatment we should get
from a victorious Germany, examine the methods the Nazis have used in dealing with Sweden,
Switzerland, and other weaker countries. A
Swedish firm which sold goods to Germany in
the period before December 1938 often was
called upon to submit a complete list of its employees. These names were checked against re-
ports from Nazi undercover agents in Sweden,
and all persons whom the Nazis considered undesirable had to be fired. Otherwise the firm
could not continue to sell to Germany. Such a

Swedish firm was required also to submit details regarding advertising accounts and promise to drop all advertising in newspapers which had carried anti-Hitler news. How could we maintain our freedom if individual American firms were compelled to discharge employees in order to win trading concessions in Europe?

What the Nazis really hope to do here is to play one section against the other. A German Foreign Office official opened his heart to me thus: "Instead of the United States we would like to deal with different areas, treating them as separate countries. We would not do much business with the country of New York, but we would buy cotton from the country of New Orleans and sell finished goods. We would buy fruit and lumber from the country of San Francisco and sell manufactured goods. We would buy packing-house and agricultural products from Chicago in exchange for our manufactured goods." You see what the Nazis really would like: to unify Europe and divide America.

It is an illusion to suppose that after the war we could get rid of our surplus agricultural commodities to a totalitarian Europe on any advantageous basis. Any products of which we had a surplus would be just the product they would not buy. For example, in the last few years the Germans put a maximum price of six cents per pound on United States cotton while at the same time they were buying cotton of inferior quality from Latin America, Africa, and Asia at nine to ten cents per pound. They did this to divert trade from this country and to put us in a more difficult trading position.

Nor could we expect to secure from Europe the products which we happened to want. We might find that all these items were on the *Verboten* list. Recently the Nazis have not been willing to sell us what we wanted to buy in the way of scientific instruments, Diesel engines, and certain types of factory installations. On the other hand, they set up a list of 253 special items — largely small handmade things like Christmas-tree ornaments and novelty goods — that we could buy, provided they were paid for in dollars and not in marks.

CHAPTER III

THE NEW ORDER IN EUROPE

1. Destruction of British People

UP to this point we have been discussing the aims and methods of the Nazis. This consideration belongs to the past and present. Can we picture the world of the future after a Nazi victory?

In estimating the possibilities of a Nazi victory, we must be guided first of all by the acts of the Nazis themselves as we know them up to the present; then, to a lesser degree, by their public statements in so far as they seem to be in line with actual policy and are not merely deceptive propaganda. Fortunately for our clear thinking, the Nazis' record is already well known. We do not have to speculate about what they will do if they win. They will certainly and surely continue the same sort of activity that has characterized them in the past. Men and movements do not change overnight. We can project into the future their probable course of action and estimate fairly accurately what sort

95

of world we shall have to live in if Hitler is the master of Europe.

First of all, a Nazi victory means a victory over Great Britain. As long as one important nation in Europe does not come to terms with Hitler and maintains a naval blockade of the European coast line, the Nazis cannot breathe; they cannot get access to the supplies or markets of the outside world. They must break through this ring of ships in order to have any real victory. The victory over Britain must be so complete that the British fleet is either destroyed, captured, or driven permanently away from its European bases. If this occurs, Britain is doomed. There are 45,000,000 people living on the British Isles today. About 80 per cent of their food comes from abroad. They have lived in the past by their international trade. Britain, situated off the continent of Europe, acted as a natural entrepôt or clearinghouse for shipping, commodity trade, and financial transactions. The British nation as a whole made its living out of trade, insurance, banking, shipping, and manufacturing for foreign countries. If Hitler wins, British trade is gone; the ports of the European continent would remain closed to her. The British Isles must shrink their populations to a figure which can be nourished from their own soil, perhaps 15,000,000 to 20,000,000 people or a little more than a third of the present number.

For the other 25,000,000 there is no hope except emigration, and they could not get away. There are not ships enough anywhere to carry such a multitude overseas before starvation would set in. This is the essential reason why the British know they are engaged in a life-and-death struggle. They cannot survive a stalemate. They must literally defeat Hitler or die, nor would there be any room in Nazi Europe for a strong and vigorous British people. Hitler has already given his most solemn warning on this point. At the close of his book, *Mein Kampf*, he has proposed a political testament for the German nation, to be its supreme guiding star of policy for the future. This contains the following words: —

The political testament of the German people for its actions abroad should be for all times as follows:

Never allow the growth of a second continental power in Europe. See in any attempt to organize a second military power on Germany's frontiers, even if it is only in the form of a state which might have military significance, an attack against Germany and see therein not only the right but the duty to prevent the growth of such a state with all means even to the use of weapons, and the duty to destroy such a state if it already exists. Take care that the strength of our people is based not upon colonies but on land in the European home territory. Never consider the empire as secure when it does not have sufficient land and territory so that every member of the race for centuries in advance may obtain his own land and never forget that the holiest right in this world is the right to own land which one can live upon himself and that the holiest sacrifice is the blood that man pours out for this land.

Hitler could have no place in his new European order for the British people. They have had too long an experience of freedom. They have too much latent energy and ability. They are too proud to make good slaves. The only possible solution which Hitler can accept would be that all that represents ability and leadership in Britain must be snuffed out. This is so essential and can be so easy. It will not be necessary to occupy all of the British Isles, but only to conquer or destroy the British fleet and then control the seas to reduce the population of Britain in a short time to manageable limits.

This is precisely the method which Hitler used to cut down the number of some of his enemies on the Continent. In November 1938, when 70,000 Jewish men were placed in concentration camps, the Nazis were willing, of course, to ransom the wealthy. Such persons were allowed to get away, provided they turned over their property and had a visa on their passport for some foreign country. But the bulk of the Jews taken in this raid were poor. No matter what pressure was applied, no funds were forthcoming. Under these circumstances, it would never do to turn them loose in Germany. It would spoil the future market for Jews to let them go unransomed. The Nazis apparently hesitated at mass executions, but found a way out of this dilemma. The Jews were lightly dressed, usually only in whatever they wore when captured, often only their pajamas. They were given hard, outdoor work to do for long hours, then forced to sleep on the ground or on beds of straw in partially open shelters, without adequate bedcovering. The natural result of this was pneumonia, which swept away so many men that the government had to enlarge the crematories which burned the remains at

Sachsenhausen, Oranienburg, and other camps.

In 1941 the Nazi solution of the Polish and Jewish population problems along the new eastern frontier is much the same. The great part of Poland is to be German and is being provided with a new set of German landlords. They need, of course, Polish laborers to operate their estates, but this number is far smaller than the existing population of the country; so the surplus Poles and Jews have been hurried out of the greater part of the country and concentrated in a limited area behind barbed wire. There has been no adequate attempt to provide food, shelter, or employment for these people. They have been dying like flies. This, of course, is what the Nazis wanted. It reapportions the population along lines which are more agreeable to them. Hitler uses the sharp weapon of starvation to prune away undesirable racial elements in his New Europe, just as a surgeon uses his knife to cut away diseased flesh.

Hitler has often stated that he does not aspire to imperialism of the old type, although to be sure the African colonial policy would seem to be an exception to this statement. He is more interested in obtaining living space for the German people, not only for the present, but according to him for centuries in advance. He wants land for the German plow in Europe, and a necessary preliminary to this must be the elimination of existing occupiers of that land. Over a temporary period Hitler will need the labor of many more slaves in Europe. Large groups of foreign workmen were brought into the Reich from Poland and Italy before the war. Since 1939 great numbers of conquered Poles, as well as Czechs, Frenchmen, Belgians, Danes, Norwegians, and Dutch, have been taken from their homes, sometimes voluntarily by the promise of food, sometimes under compulsion, and put to work in the German industrial and transportation industries.

Such men will be needed to mend road and rail connections, to repair damage from British bombers, build fortifications, improve landing fields, storage depots, and construct factories for synthetic products. Some of the better of them may be mixed with German workmen in steel mills, textile factories, or in food-preparing plants. Germany has labored toward constructing a new order with only inadequate raw materials and operating within narrow physical limits.

The substitute industries — for example, synthetic gasoline, rubber, textiles, fats, as well as the munitions factories — require immense numbers of workmen. The Germans have been working at top speed ever since the beginning of 1935 on a military program. Many of them are undoubtedly tired and more or less worn-out. Such additions as can be made to the German labor force from the conquered countries will be made.

No doubt a certain number of British can be used, although their usefulness may be more limited than that of less obstinate peoples. I fully believe that if Hitler wins by the use of starvation through the blockade, the arrest and incarceration of leading persons in Britain and the use of considerable numbers of British as slaves on the Continent will leave in the British Isles only a small population made up mostly of agricultural laborers and a small number of industrial workingmen, for example, in shipyards, a population wholly unable to maintain the continuity of British policy and British culture.

A treaty of peace with Britain seems very unlikely. For one thing, the war will go on even if the British Isles are taken. It is certain that Canada would be protected by the United States, that resistance to Hitler would still continue there, even if the British Isles fell. Undoubtedly, many persons would get away to carry on the fight from a new overseas base. They would have no reason for surrendering, and the Nazis would have a good excuse for maintaining a state of war on the remaining British. No doubt a large part of the British navy would be destroyed in the fight to prevent the Nazis from reaching Britain. It would not matter much to Hitler if a certain number of the British did escape and carried on the war from another base abroad. They could hardly operate effectively around the British Isles and draw their fuel and supplies from across the Atlantic. A food blockade of the British Isles could then be effected, whether some of the British battleships escaped to Canada or not.

When we think of the progress of the war we must not consider a defeat of Britain as just one episode in a series of disasters — it would represent the end of a chapter in human history. It would represent the end of the last effective opposition in Europe. If Britain should fall, there would be little that America could do against Hitler in his own home territory. The last base of operations against the vitals of the Reich would have vanished. The British Isles toward the end of the war will, if the United States is heavily engaged, become the landing field and taking-off point for American bombers. It is the only operating point that is vitally close to Hitler.

The fall of Britain also means the end of the Continental blockade. Within a few weeks German ships could put to sea in every direction to bring in vital materials which are now desperately missed, to carry Nazi emissaries far and wide. This would signalize that the barriers were down to totalitarianism. It would spread like a raging fire over most of the remaining areas of the world.

If Britain falls, only a few weeks need elapse until German ships going down the East and West coasts of Africa could join at Cape Town. A few divisions of German troops would be enough to break the resistance in the Dark Continent. German rule at the ports would be enough to gain the allegiance of the interior, except in the case of the English in South Africa, from whom a certain amount of resistance would be expected. If the British blockade of Europe ceases, Germany will have, together with her satellite countries, complete control of the Atlantic, the Mediterranean, the Red Sea, and the Indian Ocean. The oil of Iraq and Iran is there for the mere trouble of transporting it. The fate of India would be decided by rival pressures of Japan, Soviet Russia, and Germany. A great deal would depend upon the speed with which each one could act and the extent to which each of the three was committed elsewhere. The preferences of the Indians would not have to be consulted.

Once Britain was defeated, Hitler could commence to patch up the holes in his Continental European framework. A little intensive pressure and a minimum of actual force only would be needed to bring Switzerland and Sweden into line. A certain amount of diplomacy might have to be used on the Soviets. They are impotent to attack Germany and could not offer a serious threat at any particular point if invaded. They have their chief safety and defense in their poverty, bad roads, and vast area. Hitler would have mobilized on their frontiers and brought fear into the hearts of the wretched Russians. He might even make a bid for their continued support by generously handing out some more of Finland, although he would surely wish to keep the iron mines of Northern Sweden for himself. On account of the oil fields in Rumania, he probably would not like to give Stalin much more territory in that particular direction. Stalin can afford to be thankful for a few small grants and continue to hope that Hitler's expansion will surely bring him into opposition with America and that under the strains of his ever-widening control the Hitler menace to Russia might perhaps fall of its own weight.

2. *Economic Servitude*

In considering the new order in Europe, we need not think that all nations will be dealt with as harshly as the Poles have been handled or as the British may expect to be. The time has not yet come for the German race to inherit all the earth. Hitler's "thousand-year Reich" has still about 990 years to grow. It seems most likely that during its initial period the Nazis will tolerate, if not directly foster, the existence of satellite nationalities round about them. For one thing, these peoples need present no threat or danger. They can be separated into small states and tribal units with a good deal of cultural autonomy, resignedly working and suffering under the Nazis and postponing their aspirations for independence and self-realization indefinitely.

The Czechs have been serfs already to the Germans for three hundred years; why not a few hundred years more? The Poles have only had a brief interlude of independence to look back on. What remains of them will be scattered and beaten. In the course of the war Northern France, Holland, and Belgium will be severely battered. Starvation will be at its worst here, and these overpopulated areas will lose a large part of their present inhabitants. Those who are left will be rebellious and unwilling workers. They have not had so much training in obedience as Eastern Europeans, but a combination of force and propaganda, together with the absence of any other alternative, must make them fit into their future status in Hitler's order.

Among some of the distant and isolated peoples there may at times be greater sporadic re-

sistance, in the mountains of Norway or Yugoslavia, and at the same time greater toleration by
the Germans of racial idiosyncrasies. What harm
will it do to Hitler's new order if a few Norwegians grumble at him, so long as their fishing
boats return full-laden to German harbors?
What harm will it do to Hitler if shepherds in
the Serbian hills swear eternal enmity and pray
for the coming of a new day — they did that
under the Turks for about one thousand years —
so long as Hitler holds absolute police power over
the ports, the railways and air communications,
and the industrial centers of Europe?

Even among the Nazis there now exists considerable difference of opinion as to how the
economy of the new order is to work, and what
place the conquered peoples are to take within
it. One extreme school of thought in the National Socialist Party advocates the intensive in-
dustrialization of the Reich proper, particularly
its inner area. These elements wish to transport
industries from the periphery of Europe to its
center in order to make the Continent less vulnerable to attack from bombers which might
take off from enemy airplane carriers and in

order to put these industries in the lands with a native German population.

It is interesting to remember that this is only an enlargement of the industrial plan carried out by the Nazis inside their own country before the war. Early in 1935 they began to centralize their military construction, their new defense plants, in what they called a "safety zone," which was bordered by a semicircle starting from Bremen, swinging south of Hanover and Berlin, and north again to the Baltic. Only in the area north of this semicircle did they feel safe.

It is believed that a considerable body of the army's General Staff hold the opinion that this reshuffling of industry represents too drastic a change from the *status quo* and may defeat its purpose by the loss of efficiency in the rearrangement of the existing economic structure which the plan contemplates. Such a readjustment could only be carried out at the cost of enormous suffering for the peoples involved. It would mean several years of disorganization, added to the loss and wastage of the present war. The General Staff's idea seems to be to create around the central German Fatherland a buffer area of small semi-independent economies.

They feel that Germany cannot afford to tolerate any other large and powerful nation in Western Europe, but that she might rule as master of a group of smaller nations. If France and possibly other countries could be broken up into several parts, none of them could set up as a rival to the German overlord. Perhaps even Germany's Italian ally may be dissolved into its original component states, and Italy would once more become a mere geographic expression. In Northern and Southeastern Europe, the logical division of states is already present. None of the Scandinavian or Balkan states is large enough to be anything but Germany's vassal.

If either one of these plans works out, it will be interesting to observe how long the Nazis will keep such subject countries operating and when they may feel it necessary to fall upon one and destroy it, so that their own population and their own native economy may be enlarged. In the greatest danger are those states which directly border the Reich, because Hitler has said that he wants to broaden the European base of the German people by adding contiguous territory. Such smaller neighbors will be somewhat in the position of fowls who are kept and fed for the eggs they lay, but are finally cooked and eaten.

Nazi policy as regards this future expansion and the extension of German land ownership is still in its infancy. A curious contrast can be observed between the party policy within the old Reich, which casts envious eyes on the *Junker* landed estates and has chopped a number of them into small bits already to satisfy poor party members who wanted land, and on the other hand the party policy in Poland, which is creating new landed estates for favored members of the Nazi Party on which Polish serfs are to labor. Perhaps many of these new estates are to be cut up in turn when there are enough poor National Socialists who want farms. Time alone may tell.

As regards the frontiers of the New Europe, they will be rigidly watched. No letter, message, or package can move across without inspection and censorship. All trade of the controlled area with the outside world will be carried on through the central government in Berlin.

There will be probably no trade at all with private firms abroad, but only with other governments who make clearings or barter agreements with the Nazis. It seems likely that none of these agreements will involve payment in money, but only exchange of goods for other goods or services. Since foreign customers and suppliers will be few in number, this arrangement will be fairly simple.

Undoubtedly the central German state will act in all matters affecting the outside world for its satellites. They will have no political or commercial relations except with Germany. It seems doubtful whether their subjects will be allowed to travel abroad where they might pick up dangerous thoughts. Even the majority of the German people themselves will rarely get a chance to go outside their frontiers. The people who do go abroad will be almost exclusively representatives of the Army Services or the Propaganda Office on official government business. However, the area over which the new Germany will be master will contain such a variety of climate and scenery that there will be little need for its inhabitants to get away into a free area.

No doubt the satellite peoples will be allowed

to retain the use of their own languages, probably with German as a master speech, taught in the schools and made compulsory for all officials by law and compulsory for all business men in fact. No doubt in the whole area the German Ministry of Propaganda will maintain a close censorship of films, books, newspapers, radio broadcasts, and public meetings, just as they do today. No doubt the German Secret Police will retain their existing control over the lives of persons everywhere throughout the area.

This does not mean that the subjected peoples will be compelled to be National Socialists. They would never be allowed to join the party. The Nazi Party will comprise the aristocracy of Germany, and be as much superior to ordinary German citizens as those will be to the subject peoples. It seems doubtful whether there will be any elections held for representative bodies anywhere under German control. A certain distinction between German citizens and German subjects will no doubt be maintained. At the present time in some parts of Europe, for example Poland, there are special hotels and restaurants for citizens where Poles may not enter. Germans and Poles may share transportation upon streetcars, but the Pole enters through one door and the German through another. Of course, the Jew is not allowed to ride at all. In the New Europe, the Jew probably will soon be a thing of the past. The remnants of this unhappy people will soon disappear. Many of them have been starved, many sterilized, and it is not to be supposed that they will keep their identity much longer. One wonders what group will be selected to act as the scapegoats when the Jews are all gone.

In the New Europe money transactions will be permitted. The local subsidiary currencies may remain but their value will depend upon their relation to the master currency, the German reichsmark. The ratio will be changed from time to time as the slave peoples become more prosperous than seems necessary, in order that the Nazis can buy up their products at a cheaper rate. This procedure has been worked with success in several countries already.

Undoubtedly there will be schools in the New Europe, but they probably will not go very far beyond the elementary grades for the subject peoples. Even in Germany it is only a small number of hand-picked and reliable young peo-

114

ple who can get higher education. Fifteen thousand could go into the universities each year before the war started, of whom 10 per cent could be women. It was considered necessary to provide higher education for approximately this number in order to staff certain of the professions. The real leaders of Germany will not come from the universities, but from the leadership schools maintained by the party, which stress physical fitness, party loyalty, and fanaticism rather than intellectual capacities. The Germans are taught to think with their blood rather than their heads. Leadership is to remain the prerogative of the chosen few, and the people will be *depolitized,* a horrid Nazi word, which means that they will be kept ignorant of controversial political questions. The newspapers, books, and radio will discuss sport, music, and patriotic subjects, generally accepted party beliefs, and the weather. There shall be no wide discussion of significant public questions. This only leads to confused thinking and anarchy. If the Germans are to be held down in this rigid way, how much more barren will be the life of the slave peoples. They will live in an intellectual and cultural desert, worse even than the primitive conditions of the Middle Ages when at least the Christian Church was present everywhere to minister, to encourage, and to educate.

3. *Nazi Aristocracy*

The restriction of higher education to a small class of the ruling Germans will soon allow exact scientific and technical knowledge to die out among the slave peoples. After a generation they will be unable to use the tools of modern science as their own. They will sink into more complete dependence on the master race.

It will be interesting to see whether three types of leadership can coexist peacefully side by side in the New Germany. Present plans call for army control of a large part of the economic life of the country. The army will no doubt very largely train its own men. They will come up through cadet schools and staff colleges. According to the present setup, no member of the armed forces can be a member of the National Socialist Party so long as he wears a uniform.

The fifteen thousand youngsters who annually may enter German universities may find their number enlarged when Germany is called upon to administer an entire continent. Purely professional duties will require a large supply of doctors, scientists, laboratory technicians, engineers, and other highly trained personnel. How far can they be allowed access to dangerous and disturbing scientific knowledge? How can the party be sure of the inner loyalty of persons who are thus exposed to too much thought? A great deal may depend in the future on how army and professionally trained specialists can be made to serve an ignorant state.

The third group of leaders will serve an entirely different purpose. They are to be the young men chosen from the Hitler Youth for party loyalty, physical strength, beauty, and courage. Such youngsters are now receiving specialized leadership training in three almost monastic institutions, one at Crossensee in Pomerania, one in the Eifel Mountains, and one in Algäu. Such schooling as they get is hardly from books. They must become good at fencing, boxing, skiing, swimming, diving, riding. They must be skilled aviators, parachute jumpers, crack shots with the rifle and revolver, and hardened to meet any emergency. They are to be free from fear and so worthy to lead others. They must be fanatically loyal to Hitler and the Nazi movement and imbued with the idea of the master race and their chosen privilege as leaders. This group will not be burdened by conscientious doubts and inner troublings of the spirit. They will be more likely to be hardboiled supergangsters, dangerous to the movement unless they are overpaid. Can these three groups get along among themselves? Can they reconcile their differing points of view in a common loyalty to the new superstate? This remains to be seen.

It seems clear that the New Europe will have a new religion. Hitler is fanatic on the point of uniting his people in a common religious bond which shall end the schism between Catholic and Protestant and bring all of his people of German blood into the German church. Whether this church will have any real ties with the Christian faith remains problematical. There are two religious movements within the National Socialist Party. One group would retain the Christian beliefs after eliminating the Old Testament, revising the New Testament, and interpreting the historic figure of Christ in new and strange lights. The softer virtues of the New

118

Testament are passed over. The Sermon on the Mount and the Beatitudes have no place in this faith. There is to be no turning of the other cheek or loving your neighbor as yourself.

The other religious movement in the party is more thorough and admits that it is frankly pagan. Such religious leaders, which include Rosenberg, the official party philosopher, and Von Schirach, the leader of the Hitler Youth, wish to throw out the entire body of Christian traditions and beliefs. They feel that the German race made a historic mistake when it was persuaded to adopt the decadent Christian faith of a dying Roman Empire. They would return to the indigenous and healthy paganism characteristic of Nordic Germans and evolved out of their own inner consciousness. Even the majority of the Nazi Party do not yet embrace such an extreme doctrine, not to speak of the rank and file of Germans in general. But the influence of the party press, of the party books and periodicals, and the ceaseless pressure upon the youth, may bring about a changed attitude.

It is clear that the conflict between the National Socialist movement and the Christian Church has sharpened and deepened in recent years. No concordat or other agreement can disguise this fact. Hitler, I feel, welcomes this conflict, although as far back as 1923 he broke with Ludendorff over the question of openly acknowledging the pagan religion. In his heart Hitler hates Christianity for its universality, its weakening doctrines of pity, humility, and brotherhood. Hitler wants to see his people make their feelings of patriotism and loyalty their religion. The real God of the future is to be the State, the race, with Hitler as its prophet. No doubt semi-divine honors will be paid to the Fuehrer after his death. I feel sure he is already enjoying them in anticipation. German women have been instructed to adorn a corner of their best room with a picture or bust of Hitler, and they are encouraged to place lighted candles or fresh flowers in front of it every day, meanwhile reciting a scrap of Nazi poetry or a phrase from *Mein Kampf*. This is the beginning of a new idolatry similar to the worship of Lenin and Stalin by Soviet peasants. There is only one god, Germany, and Hitler is his prophet. In many ways Hitler reminds us of Mohammed.

Already a goodly number of ancestor temples throughout the Reich have been set up to take the place of Christian churches. They usually consist of a semicircle of pillars standing under the sky, with a bust of Hitler in the center and a place for the congregation in the front. There is plentiful ornamentation of the swastika but very little other symbolism. Here are performed newly evolved services of Nazi marriage, Nazi christening, and Nazi burial. Rosenberg in his *Myth of the Twentieth Century* suggests that in the future loyal Germans will gather on Sundays and holidays around war memorials to the dead, in German towns and villages, and there conduct patriotic services which will replace former religious observances. Such worship of the state is similar to the Shinto religion of Japan, strongly reminiscent of the religion of the Roman Empire, with its shadowy gods, its deification of the emperor, and real worship of the state.

4. Rebuilding Europe on Nazi Lines

A further point of comparison between the New Germany and the Empire of Rome will be the far-flung network of roads and the fast communication system leading from the frontiers to the capital. Hitler is mad about fast transportation. Planes, cars, speedways, and streamlined trains, all have been fostered under his rule. The New Europe will be crisscrossed by super auto highways strategically located and running to the farthest points of Hitler's empire. Such roads will be four-lane highways with grade crossings eliminated, clover-leaf entrances and exits, controlled by military police and with no upper speed limits. The only speed limit now on such highways in Germany is the poor material in German automobiles which tends to burn out at sustained high speeds. I have seen many a German car forced to leave the road for such reasons or because of a vapor lock in the carburetor, due to the 15 per cent mixture of alcohol in the gasoline.

Such German super auto highways date back to Hitler's May Day speech of 1933. They were originally built straight as arrows toward the frontiers in every direction. Then, as the frontiers have been pushed back, the roads have been lengthened. I remember in 1937 a signpost near a crossing outside of Berlin which gave the exact distance in kilometers along the new roads to a number of points. It was, for example, just 1000 kilometers to Paris by this new road. Paris has duly been conquered, and the road no doubt will soon reach there. It was a common joke in Berlin during those days that the roads would soon run to Cape Town, Calcutta, and Peking.

The Nazis are frequently told of their opportunities for the extension of railway communications toward the south and east. They will extend the Berlin–Bagdad road to India. They will run their trains from Berlin down along the East and West coasts of Africa, tunneling under the Straits of Gibraltar and the Bosporus. They will finally achieve what British and French impotence has unduly postponed — a tunnel under the English Channel. They will utilize extension bridges between the Danish Islands and a new bridge or tunnel near Copenhagen to send through trains by land to Norway and Sweden. Fast rail and road transportation will link Europe, Asia, and Africa into an economic and political unit it has never known. The Nazis plan to deepen existing rivers and canals so that fair-sized steamers can proceed from the Rhine through the Danube to the Black Sea, from the Baltic into the Rhine and Danube. They plan air transportation on a mass scale. The new chief air field at Tempelhof, Berlin, is the most stupendous airport in existence: a huge semicircle of steel forming an apron under which 100 planes can enter and leave simultaneously; the semicircle is over a mile long. It is anchored by a whole series of eight-story buildings on the convex side. These buildings are to house aviation employees and even now provide office space for at least 100,000 persons. The strange thing about all this is the fact that practically no one in Central Europe can afford to fly except persons on government business, but there will be no lack of such air passengers — the Nazis will see to that.

Hitler is not only the greatest military chief in history, he aspires to be known as the greatest builder of the ages. Ever since he failed of admission to the architectural school in Vienna, he has cherished his plans for rebuilding everything, no matter what, particularly if it was on a huge scale. He has been constructing at Nuremberg a stadium to hold 400,000 people. Just outside is the Zeppelin field with accommodations for 1,500,000. He has announced the future construction of an avenue of triumph between

Berlin and Munich to be flanked on both sides by statues representing Germany's heroes. There may be enough of them to line the road on both sides if the war persists much longer.

This will make the Kaiser's Victory Avenue, lined with effigies of Hohenzollern Princes for two blocks long, seem puny. Incidentally, Hitler has moved away the Hohenzollern statues already to make room for his own improvements. In central Berlin he has started to construct vast north–south and east–west axes. For much of their length these avenues are to be more than one hundred yards wide — about the width of a city block. At each end of the north–south axis is to be constructed a huge railway station. Many superbuildings line these avenues, either planned or under way.

The River Spree was unfortunately in the way, but Hitler is going to move the river; at least he has said so. In Hamburg, on the other hand, he is going to allow the River Elbe to remain; but he plans to build a super-Brooklyn Bridge over it, with skyscraper towers sixty-five stories high at each end. These plans are, of course, subject to many revisions. Hitler changes his mind frequently. He loves nothing better than to sprawl over huge maps, sketching in buildings at various points and rubbing them out again. In 1937 he constructed a new central office building to house the chancellery and staff. In the spring of 1938 he changed his mind, tore it down, and had it built again according to a different plan. Hitler at first hoped to make Munich his capital city, but in recent years he has apparently veered toward continuing Berlin as the center; at least his elaborate construction plans there lead to this belief.

However, he has his own private capital city at Berchtesgaden, where he has a large estate in the mountains, including a retreat on the top of one peak with a glassed-in veranda all around and its only entrance an elevator shaft reached by a tunnel in the heart of the mountain. Perhaps now that the Reich has extended its frontiers, this small mountain will not be high enough; and a new eagle's nest for the Fuehrer will be constructed at a still loftier altitude.

Other Nazi leaders are not far behind their chief. Goering has built his home at Karinhall to the north of Berlin in a wooded area, miles away from the highroad. All oncoming cars must pass through two covered approaches where

sensitive photoelectric cells register the movement of vehicles, so that bells ring, whistles
blow, and the soldiers are alarmed in the guard-
house. A few moments later such vehicles are
surrounded on the road by squads of motor-
cycle police who dash out from the woods on
both sides, carefully survey the car and its occupants, and make the necessary inspections. I
never could decide whether this was considered
necessary or whether it was simply practice
training for the German military police. A state
visitor to Goering's home is welcomed by pet
lion cubs and a squad of trumpeters blaring
an operatic salute from Wagner.

When Goering entertained the delegates to the
International Chamber of Commerce in 1937,
he used the Kaiser's palace for the occasion. He
dispensed with electric lights and illuminated
the rooms, stairways, and courtyards by double
lines of footmen dressed in red livery and carrying torches. Only the Emperor Nero would
have felt thoroughly at home on such an occasion.

The next day Goebbels staged a party on
Peacock Island near Potsdam, which should
outdo Goering's splendor. He had built a bridge

127

of boats to connect the island with the shore. After crossing this bridge, where incidentally traffic was interrupted for a while because a fire engine supplied by the City of Berlin broke through and fell into the water, we were led to island paths marked off in the dusk by girls and young women from the gymnastic schools of Germany. They were all dressed in white silk tights and carried long white wands held perpendicularly. Passing by hundreds of these damsels, we finally arrived at the bar where free drinks, served all night by fifty bartenders over a bar perhaps fifty yards long, turned melancholy into wine and song. Passing onward through paths of hothouse flowers, lighted by concealed colored searchlights and varied with newly laid fountains, we arrived at the dance floor directly in the middle of an immense park. The overhead light was from forty thousand Japanese lanterns. The whole decorations cost roughly from $150,000 to $200,000.

A thousand waiters served lobster, caviar, saddle of venison, as many delicacies as one could think of. As one American observer remarked to me, "Only a bankrupt nation could afford to splurge like that." The Nazis, you can see, are touched with megalomania. They understand tactics of overpowering, sensuous, spectacular display. It can be assumed that all their planning for the New Europe will be colored by this tendency.

The German people are longing for the day when the war will be over and the boys can come home. The war may someday be over, but if the boys come home it will not be to stay for long. The German army will not be demobilized after the war. It will remain quartered upon the conquered peoples and especially will be strung along the coast and the Eastern frontiers. Germany is building military barracks and concentration camps of dressed stone and re-enforced concrete, with sometimes stained-glass windows in the officers' quarters. These edifices are built to last for a goodly portion of the thousand-year Reich. They are not going to be emptied of occupants. The Nazi army will be a permanent fixture. All German boys will pass through it and will probably remain in it for long periods. Like the Roman legions which kept watch on the frontiers of the empire for five hundred years, the Nazis will keep their forces together to retain their hold upon subjugated peoples.

A suitable source of long-term enlistments will be the families of the hereditary peasants, who cannot leave the land except for military service. The oldest son must take the farm upon his father's death. The younger sons may either go into the armed forces as a permanent career or may later be given tracts of land seized from conquered peoples, just as the legionnaires of Rome were pensioned off with farms and settled in dangerous areas where they could quickly be called to the colors.

As I see it, the future German rule will rest upon the authority of a semi-divine Fuehrer, and around him will be a group of selected leaders of the Reich. Only this group will have their hands on the source of power. They will have at their disposal a reservoir of trained scientists, technicians, and propagandists. Below this group there will be no higher education or scientific training. Modern knowledge will remain a complete monopoly of the rulers and will not filter down through to the masses. Below the educated classes will come a vast reservoir of skill and energy from the trained German people. They will be provided with jobs. They will have more than enough to do, and they will be guaranteed

130

a standard of living superior to the subject peoples. Their task will be to operate industry, agriculture, and transportation. Mingled with this group, drawn from it, and returning to it, will be the armed forces composed of German citizens.

Below all Germans will come the slave peoples, whose lot it will be to perform simple and low-paid tasks involving little specialized training. They can perform routine operations in mass-production industry; they can do heavy manual labor or work on the estates of their German masters. After only a very few years they will be forever deprived of their opportunity of effective revolt. All control over manufacture and operation of airplanes, motor vehicles, locomotives, ships, and other means of rapid transportation, all manufacture of weapons, explosives, and scientific instruments, will be in the hands of their masters. A slave people may manufacture food or weapons suitable for an uprising in the Middle Ages; but they cannot by any coup seize the centers of production of modern mechanized weapons. They will be as ineffective for modern war as the Navahos on an Indian reservation.

After this system becomes once firmly es-

tablished, after the present generation of Frenchmen, Dutchmen, and Czechs has passed military
age, coming generations will lack all the means,
whether intellectual or material, for making an
effective stand against the Germans. Of course,
they may murder one now and again on some
dark night, but that will simply be an occupational hazard in the German army, and will not
be of serious consequence. Any attempt from
outside Europe to release the defeated peoples
will have to come before this system gets really
under way. That means it will have to come as
a part of the present war. We dare not allow Hitler much breathing space to convert his armies
of conquest into armies of effective occupation.
The Nazis have grasped the fact that by mo-
nopolizing modern science and technique for
themselves they have a more decisive advantage
over weaker peoples than did ever the Roman
legions with their short swords and cowhide
shields. The airplane and the tank are the modern equivalents of the medieval knights in armor,
a few of whom could control a large country-
side of grumbling yokels armed with staves and
cudgels.

The chief and ever-recurring danger for such

a system does not arise from the bottom, but in decay and discontent at the top. The history of most military dictatorships or Oriental empires of the distant past has been a history of palace revolutions and family squabbles. Government by the Praetorian guards, poisonings by cast-off favorites, and intrigue in high places — all these empires have been rotten at the top. They have often rested upon the loyalty of vast millions of naïve and uninformed citizenry. But loyalty and self-sacrifice do not flourish amid the Byzantine atmosphere of a dictator's court. As I write, we do not know why Hess made his incredible flight to Scotland. We can remember that in 1934 Hitler killed between twelve and thirteen hundred of his close associates as part of a struggle for control of the Nazi machine. Going back further we can remember that in 1926 Goebbels and Gregor Strasser staged a revolt to get rid of Hitler as the Fuehrer and put themselves in his place. We can remember the intrigues which surrounded such Nazi leaders as Papen, Ribbentrop, and Henlein. All of them saw their closest associates assassinated or imprisoned.

It used to be a common saying in Berlin that

the Secret Police already possessed signed affidavits and other documents, including photographs, which would certainly prove the guilt of any big Nazi who was worth eliminating. Usually those charges were either homosexuality or graft. All Hitler and his Chief of Police Himmler had to do was to call for the files, and they could frame anybody that they wished on short notice. Much of this evidence was no doubt true; if not, then the Gestapo is inventive and resourceful enough to supply any needed deficiencies. Himmler knows where the body is buried in every case. No doubt other top Nazis have the goods on Himmler if it ever comes to that.

5. Co-operation between Dictatorships

The economic organization of the New Europe must necessarily be centralized in Berlin. Nazi planned economy must extend over the whole area which Hitler proposes to dominate. He cannot allow deviations from his usual rulings without danger of disorganizing his whole

134

system. The experience of the last few years shows that economic planning and a system of free enterprise cannot permanently endure side by side in the same nation. For example, the Nazi system of wage and price control must be extended to every area which they dominate, otherwise the control of prices would soon get out of line. If labor is compulsory in some areas, it must be made so everywhere or else laborers will migrate to freer regions. At the frontiers there must be a uniform system of handling foreign trade and foreign exchange. Otherwise holes might develop at certain points through which capital might drain out of the country.

All this means that economic planning must be made on a Continental scale. All transactions with the outside world must pass through a central bureaucracy, probably the German Ministry of Economics. All financial transactions must be lined up under the German Ministry of Finance and the Reichsbank. In recent months a European clearing system for financial transactions has been proclaimed. Production, consumption, transportation, and finance will be handled from Berlin for the entire area, extending from the North Cape in the Land of the Midnight Sun to the tip of South Africa, with possible extension into Asia, which is yet undefined. This will give Hitler a block of, let us say, five hundred to eight hundred million people, or even more if he can include India in his scheme of operations. This block will border directly on the Soviet Union — a frontier running from somewhere in Scandinavia until it meets the warm waters of the Indian Ocean. A common frontier several thousand miles long.

The Soviet Union will be decidedly a junior partner, smaller in population and resources, infinitely weaker in mechanical efficiency and administrative control. The German block will be constantly in a position to assert political, economic, and military pressure upon its neighbor. The probable relations between these two similar but rival economies form a fascinating field for speculation. At present they are bound together by a common desire to weaken the Western democratic nations, to break down the capitalistic system and prepare the world for a new order. But the systems, though similar, are competitive. Both are run by cynical, opportunistic adventurers who think first and only in terms of power politics. There can be no permanent understanding between them. Revolutions do not compromise; they attack, although they may sometimes pause to gather strength for a fresh onslaught.

There is no question of an attack by Soviet Russia on Germany under existing circumstances. German strength is much too great. There is, however, a speculative possibility that Hitler might decide to attack Russia. There is no physical reason why he could not succeed in such a movement. The Soviet army is numerous, it possesses an abundance of mechanical equipment of only moderate efficiency; but it lacks training and leadership, it has no effective means of transportation. There is no doubt in the world but that Hitler could drive his army into Soviet territory and reach any objective he might select. Russia's greatest protection now is its poverty, the fact that an attack on Soviet territory could hardly be made to pay. In the last war German troops held the Ukraine for two summers, in 1917 and 1918, but they only succeeded in bringing out 43,000 small carloads of grain. This was a very poor return for the expense of the whole operation.

Russia of course has tremendous natural resources, but they are still for the most part un-developed. It seems to me that the Germans will turn their time and attention to areas which they can secure with less opposition and receive a greater return. As a consequence of a success-ful struggle with Britain, they will surely have areas available for exploitation which will yield a greater economic return.

Hitler may not mean to invade Soviet Russia. He may be able to infiltrate it with German technicians and engineers, gradually to draw the two areas close together in economic co-opera-tion. He should be strong enough to persuade Stalin to abandon any ties he may have with nations hostile to Germany. He can assume the position of exclusive stewardship over the So-viet's dealings with the Western Hemisphere, and little by little bring the whole Soviet block into his orbit. This might even be done without war, by economic and political high-pressure tactics. Stalin's seat in the Kremlin is uncomfortably hot. He has been forced to liquidate most of the old Communists and an appalling number of the officers in the Soviet army. One third of all the Communist Party has been purged since 1937 and one half of all the Comsomols have been thrown out for one reason or another. The attraction of a more powerful economy and an invincible army may spread treason widely through Soviet officialdom. After all, their efficiency and standard of living are well below those of the German block. They may feel that closer co-operation with Hitler means better living standards for the Soviet people and an assurance that their regime will not be destroyed from below.

Stalin's hope, on the other hand, must be that the war will continue, with weakening both of National Socialist Germany and of its democratic opposition, so that the Soviet will be relatively strengthened. However, I feel that, even weakened and defeated, Germany would be strong enough to prevent seizure of its home territories by Soviet troops. In this association of double-crossing rivals, Hitler now has most of the advantages on his side.

So far little mention has been made of Japan's new order in Asia. Obviously no one knows whether Germany, Soviet Russia, and Japan will be able to keep the peace among themselves and follow their common policy of aggression against what remains of a free world. Probably none of the leaders in the three totalitarian capitals knows himself just how the future will work out; but this is certain — we must prepare for the worst. We must take into account the possibility that these three bandit nations can achieve a measure of effective collaboration and continue to synchronize their aggressive acts in such a way as to cause us the maximum of embarrassment and danger. We dare not afford to rely upon a falling-out among thieves, not even if they simulate a good deal of controversy. I believe that these three robber states can at least temporarily find a common accord in their intention to expand their areas of control and loot their neighbors. Even supposing the Japanese do fall out with Hitler someday, they may postpone this until after they have finally settled accounts with us. It would be dangerous for the United States if we fail to allow for the possibility of a concerted and sustained attack upon North America by all these totalitarian groups, assisted by all the slaves, vassals, and stooges they can muster anywhere in the world. We should expect if Hitler wins that any controversy in which we might engage would be timed by him to coincide with similar pressure applied by Japan across the

Pacific. Our troubles would never come singly. We should have no free nations to whom to turn; we should have only our own strength to rely upon.

Our enemies would have under their flags 80 to 90 per cent of the human race. They would command the oceans outside the zone of our effective naval and air patrol near our shores. American citizens who ventured into Asia, Europe, or Africa would do so at their peril. We should have to be a whole nation of "Minutemen," ready to rush to arms at the first sign of invasion. Our children could not, of course, expect to enjoy "a better world" under such conditions.

6. *The Scientific Slave State*

Just how far could the Nazis succeed in introducing their economic, military, and political system over Europe, Africa, and part of Asia? I feel that given time they could achieve a stability which might be unbroken for a long period to come. As soon as German armies have put down opposition, once the Secret Police have removed dissenters and the concentration camps have received the rebellious, the first battle has been won. There will no doubt be a tremendous amount of human suffering and misery over the entire area, but it will not be able to express itself effectively. The Nazis will be able to use their satellite governments as pliable tools to secure uniformity and regimentation throughout the area. The Nazis will control supplies of food, clothing, and money. Noncompliance with their orders will mean starvation. Most people must submit and take their allotted place in the regime. I foresee an era of vast construction enterprises: the rebuilding of bombed cities; the relocation of industry within Central Germany and construction of immense plants for the manufacture of ersatz and other products; the construction of thousands of miles of railway and motor highways; the building of planes and ships.

If Hitler succeeds in driving the British out of Africa, which ought not to take very long once Britain is defeated in her home territory, we may see Germans' feverish exploitation of the Rand Gold Mines and the South African diamond deposits. These products may have some value in dealings with the rest of the world, or might presage the reintroduction of a gold reserve behind the German reichsmark and a supply of industrial diamonds for the machine-tool and aviation industries.

The first few years of conquest would be the hardest. Every additional year of peace would permit the Nazis to extend their systems of training and discipline over the subjugated peoples. The children would be taught new versions of history in the elementary schools. They would be carefully insulated from contact with the outer world. In another generation Hitler would have a passive and acquiescent population which had lost its hope, though not its love, of liberty. I see no reason why a new Caesarism could not be maintained by these methods just as effectively as the Roman emperors held together their subject populations for nearly five hundred years. If the administration at the top continued to be farsighted and severe, they could reintroduce the proved technique and practices of ancient Oriental despotisms, refined by modern knowledge and sharpened by modern science. The scientific slave state on a Continental scale is not a dream. It is taking shape before our very eyes.

Some critics may allege that economic difficulties will cause such widespread dissension that the regime must fall of its own weight. Such critics have consistently prophesied the early collapse of the Soviet experiment. They were correct in asserting that Soviet economy was operating badly, but that fact failed to shatter the strength of the Soviet state. In 1936 and subsequent years Stalin decided forcibly to remove the Russian peasants from their small farms and place them on giant collective farms, where they lost the ownership of their land, livestock, and much of their personal property. It is well known how the Ukrainian peasants resisted and how the Red army was sent in to collect all food supplies, so that after a large number, estimated at between six and seven million persons, died of starvation, the remainder were placed upon the collective farms. It is true that they went sullenly, but this did not matter to the Kremlin. That loss in population was made up by the increase of births over deaths in two years.

In the same way Hitler will not be unduly disturbed if there is widespread resistance to his agents in the conquered countries. It will simply prove to be the worse for the discontented; they will lose their meal tickets and soon pass out of the picture. In a totalitarian system, a shortage of food and other necessary supplies strengthens the all-powerful control of the central authorities, because they hold the power of life and death in their hands. Americans are sometimes inclined to estimate the probable conduct of foreign peoples by their own psychological reactions to dictatorial methods. But this is an error in thinking. We must not assume that the peoples of Europe, Asia, and Africa have been accustomed to place the same importance on the liberty of the individual or that they resent in the same degree as we should infringements on their own rights. Many of them have never been fully free. They would quickly appreciate freedom if they once tasted it, but they will soon become too dulled even to think much about it.

We can expect wide variation in the reactions of differing racial groups. I can believe that the Nazis will have to handle the Bedouin Arabs of the desert with much greater tact and diplomacy than they will need in forcing their regulations upon the hungry working populations of peaceful European cities or the good-natured natives of Central Africa. Let us remember that the Nazi system is an elastic one which can improvise new policies and accommodate itself to any and all circumstances. The Nazis will not be bothered by charges of inconsistency; their one essential aim is to seize power and hold it. The effective means of doing so will be the proper means in their eyes. They can adopt whatever tactics are suitable in a particular area and alter them when circumstances change.

For example, while they have been persecuting the Catholic Church in Germany, they used the same church as an instrument of their policy in Slovakia to break up the Czech state. They are not troubled by preconceived ideas or precise definitions. They do not have a Marxian dialectic or a Westminster catechism. Even Hitler's *Mein Kampf* and the *Twenty-five Points of the National Socialist Party Program*, announced in the year of 1920, can be reinterpreted to mean whatever the party leaders wish them to mean to suit the occasion. Nazi authorities have already hundreds of different definitions for Socialism. A common German saying runs as follows: "There is only one National Socialist — Hitler. He is the only one who knows what it means."

This flexibility would prove to be an enormous advantage in dealing with new situations. For example, Hitler has already proclaimed that there are no outward physical characteristics to identify Nordic Germans. They can only be properly classified on the basis of their inner feelings and actions. The Nazis have no scruples and no inhibitions. They cannot be dissuaded from any course of action by mere words. It does no good to accuse them of wickedness or crime. One of their favorite tactics in the past was to shock conventionally-minded Germans into complete paralysis of thought and action by admitting the truth of criticism and bragging that they were worse than anybody had imagined. All weapons of argument lose their effectiveness against the gleeful cynicism of Dr. Goebbels.

Shortly after the blood purge of June 30, 1934, Goebbels made a public speech in which he pointed out that the extinction of many innocent persons could be considered a gain for the Nazi movement; for the shedding of innocent blood made the cause more holy. This came from a man who was implicated in the murder of between 1200 and 1300 persons. Such an idea seems a throwback to the old belief in human sacrifice.

CHAPTER IV

HITLER REACHES OUT TO THE NEW WORLD

1. Sale of Arms to Latin America

WE have seen how the fall of Britain would mean the rapid extension of Nazi power over all Europe, Africa, and part of Asia; how a huge scientific slave state could be erected upon the helpless, though unwilling people of the conquered nations; how this new European order would become the senior partner in a working agreement with the Soviet system and the Japanese, until further notice. Could we not, however, live by ourselves across the ocean barriers that separate the Old World from the New? Could we not draw imaginary lines from pole to pole in both oceans and preserve the twenty-one American republics in a self-contained democratic block? The answer to this is, "No!"

Hitler would undoubtedly be kept very busy after the defeat of Britain in consolidating his Old World power, but he has numbers of agents throughout the Americas who would not be needed in the Old World and could keep on doing what they are doing now — preparing the way for Hitlerism on this side of the water. Some three million Germans live in Latin America. Many of them now are avowed agents of the Nazis. Many more would join the movement as soon as Hitler's success in Europe seemed certain. One third of the population of Argentina is Italian, many more Italians live in other Latin-American states. The culture, language, religion, and governmental structures of Latin America do not come from Anglo-Saxon roots, but from the Latin nations of Southern Europe — Spain, Portugal, France, and Italy. Every one of these countries would be included in the New Hitler State. Every influence they could bring to bear upon Latin-American republics would be placed at Hitler's disposal. In addition, Europe has been the market for the bulk of Latin-American products. An average value of $1,200,000,000 worth of these goods went to European consumers every year, or twice the amount usually shipped to North America. Such products are now piled up in warehouses awaiting possible customers. How can we prevent Latin-American exporters from shipping goods to Hitler, who will offer to buy everything in sight? How can

152

we prevent Hitler from buying Latin-American products which he will desire? Some persons may say, "But Europe will be so disorganized that it will have nothing to send in exchange." I want to point out that Hitler will have one sort of commodities which the Latin-American states will desire above all things — *arms*. Germany at the conclusion of this war, if she is victorious, will have worn out her peacetime industries, but she will possess an expanded plant capacity for the production of battleships, cruisers, and submarines, bombers and fighting planes, machine guns, revolvers, and rifles, armored cars and tanks. The triumph of force in Europe will be the signal for every Latin-American nation to be armed. They will fear revolution from within and aggression from without. The German war equipment, wearing the blue ribbon of victory, is bound to be rated the best in the world, and it would be offered at attractive prices in enormous quantities. It is certain to be snapped up by Latin-American republics, waiting anxiously to get rid of surplus raw products. If just one nation in South America decides to rearm with Hitler's equipment, there is no doubt that its neighbors will be quick to do the same. This is no mere dream. It is a continuation of the tactics which the Nazis have already used successfully for years before the war. They continually armed their small neighbors. The export of war equipment was one of Germany's best trading assets.

Some may say that the Nazis would not sell arms to potential enemies, because of the fear of building up too much strength against themselves. They have never shown any disinclination to do this in the past. Confident of their own overwhelming superiority, sure that they can retain the latest and most effective types of weapons, they gladly export secondhand military equipment, or even some of the best for the right prices. In fact, they are glad to arm their possible enemies because this leaves them the power of control over ammunition and replacements. In the recent campaign against Yugoslavia and Greece, for example, both those nations had been chiefly equipped with German war materials. The advancing German soldiers were killed by their own German bullets, but this was all a part of Hitler's game. He doesn't seem to mind. The Greek army was outfitted with war materials seized from the Austrians when Hitler took control of Vienna in the spring of 1938.

Yugoslavia had been armed both from Germany and from Czechoslovakia, but had paid for the weapons in essential raw materials which were worth more to Hitler than the lives of some of his soldiers.

It may be argued that the South American nations will be outfitted through our own American defense program, but if Hitler wins in Europe we shall need nearly every plane and every gun that we can make at home. We may perhaps retain the business of certain Latin-American states in these commodities, but certainly not all of them. It may be argued that the Good Neighbor Policy and better relations between the American republics in recent years will cause them all to maintain a solid front against Hitler's wiles. This overlooks the fact that even before Hitler has won complete victory in Europe, even while the contest remains undecided, a number of Latin-American states, whom perhaps it is not tactful to single out by name, have shown unmistakable signs that they favor co-operation with the Axis and show suspicion of too close relations with North America. Already they seem to have decided which is the stronger of the opposing forces and on which side their bread is buttered. The Nazis at this moment have the inside track in several Latin-American countries, including Panama, the guardian of the Canal.

There are a great number of reasons why Latin-American nations feel moved in this direction. Many of them are political dictatorships with only an outward façade of democracy. They feel a strong affinity toward the authoritarian forms of government. In many of these states there are individual problems of racial antagonism, and so Nazi doctrines of racial superiority form a welcome bulwark to the rule of white aristocracy in countries where there are large Indian, Negro, and mestizo populations. Aside from the strong pull of economic forces which draws them into the Axis orbit, many Latin-American states still cherish suspicions toward their stronger neighbor of the North. They resent our long self-satisfied assumption of political, economic, and even moral superiority. They are tired of living in a world of Anglo-Saxon leadership and would be glad to try something else for a change. That this change might be for the worse is apparent only to an intelligent minority.

Let us not forget that North Americans have gone to South America on business only. They have remained within their exclusive circles, patronized exclusive clubs; never, for the most part, have they married Latin-American women or adopted the language of the countries where they domiciled. The German, Italian, Spanish, Portuguese immigrants have come to Latin America to make it their home. They have intermingled and adopted local customs and languages and come far closer to the hearts of the people than we have ever done. I believe that a Hitler victory over Great Britain would be signalized by a succession of Nazi-inspired revolutions in Latin-American countries, exploding like a packet of firecrackers. In many of these countries there exist a military dictatorship and a potential military opposition. If the present government does not come around promptly, the Nazis can negotiate with the opposition, supply them with arms and equipment, finance a sudden *coup d'état,* and obtain power in this way. Such occurrences are not rare in Latin-American history.

Nazi-sponsored revolutions have occurred in several countries already, generally quickly put down, but only because they were premature, like the uprising of 1934, where overenthusiastic Austrian Nazis anticipated Hitler's time-table, killed Prime Minister Dollfuss, seized the central radio station, and would have succeeded, except for the fact that Mussolini at that time was not yet an Axis partner. Already in Brazil the president-dictator has been besieged in his own palace by Nazi-inspired revolutionists. In Chile and in Uruguay such movements have resulted in violence. A German victory would insure more activity of the same kind. Does anyone believe that these putsches would all fail or that the Nazis would not be able to secure a foothold in the South American Continent at some point?

The United States cannot maintain a naval patrol all the way through the Atlantic and the Pacific. We cannot enforce a blockade of Europe, Asia, and Africa. We cannot call out the Marines to stop Mussolini from sending his daughter on a friendly visit to the president of a Latin-American republic, bringing with her baggage fifty disguised military and aviation experts to start the training of Nazi Bunds under assumed names. We cannot forbid revolutions in South America — at least we have never been able to in the past. We cannot actively interfere in the internal politics of the Latin-American republics to oppose Nazi plans without often arousing the resentment of the country concerned and of its neighbors, and thus bringing about the very condition which we hoped to prevent.

No, it is not possible that the totalitarian tide can be successfully held back from moving across the South Atlantic. We must abandon the belief that we can isolate all the New World from a victorious Germany.

2. *Sowing Trouble in the Americas*

Another line of opinion favors an American defense of the quarter-sphere. That means the defense block in the Western Hemisphere north of the Equator, or a stretch of territory roughly so bounded. A defense line running across the north of South America would involve a good many difficulties. We have yet to receive permission from South American states to set up naval or air bases anywhere in that continent. Military operations in that area would be carried out only under terrible handicaps. The equatorial climate, native diseases, tropic heat, torrential rains, fast-growing vegetation, present many obstacles to us just as to the enemy. Both sides would have to work under difficulties. I can hardly believe that the future is going to see armies operating in the South American jungles as part of hemisphere defense.

Far more likely will there be a continuance of economic pressure working from south to north in the Western republics. Most observers believe that there exists a good deal of latent hostility between Latin-American countries; that it might be very easy to play upon the suspicions, rivalries, and jealousies down there and bring about an actual separation of the continent into two opposing camps. Some commentators even have been bold enough to choose sides already. They usually list Argentina as heading one camp and Brazil the other. There is no general agreement as to just how other states might line up under the banner of these main opponents. The Nazis would be in their element in promoting antagonism of this kind. They could play both sides simultaneously and finally pick the one that promised to be the most useful. Incidentally, they could sell plenty of equipment in the process. The Gran Chaco War would only be a skirmish compared to the conflict which might be provoked right in Latin America itself. Once trouble of this kind started, there would be plenty of excuses for keeping it going and lining up the adversaries on both the East and the West Coast.

In some such manner Nazi agents might come to acquire military bases within striking distance of the Canal Zone and would be in a position to put considerable pressure on one after another of the little countries of Central America. Plenty of German and other totalitarian agents are in this area today. They already have far-reaching plans and a broad vista of miscellaneous avenues of approach to this general situation. Wherever and whenever we draw a deadline, we can be accused of imperialism and exploitation of smaller neighbors. Berlin can stress racial antagonisms or sympathies in the familiar Nazi way, or may turn around and use a Communist approach to underprivileged natives, or both these methods and others may all be applied simultaneously. There seems to be the possibility that such tactics might have considerable success throughout Mexico and as far as the line of the

Rio Grande. Apparently no one can say for sure just what shade of red represents the majority opinion in Mexico today, but Berlin is good at matching colors.

How can an America organized for peace frame a long-term military policy which can successfully counteract these tactics throughout Latin America? We have no love for military expeditions; we have no secret propaganda and corruption funds. We have stood for a policy of freedom of action and expression for the individual, which makes airtight control over these regions contrary to our habits of thought and action. The Nazis all along the line have an advantage in their type of tactics. For example, they can threaten private individuals and their families with present or future punishment if they are anti-Nazi. We would not wish to stoop to these tactics. The Nazis compile lists of their friends and enemies all over the world. Latin Americans are naturally reluctant to be listed in Berlin's black book. The Latin American who champions Hitler now is in no particular danger of reprisal if Hitler loses, but anyone who opposes Hitler knows what to expect if the Nazis ever do win. The risks are unevenly distributed. To appear sympathetic with the totalitarians is simply a form of life and property insurance which many a prudent Latin American takes out under existing circumstances.

Just how far in Latin America the Nazis now plan to extend their sway is a matter of dispute. I have seen Nazi maps which illustrate a difference of opinion on this point. Some maps of the future world give Germany control to the quarter-sphere, some to the Panama Canal, some to the Rio Grande, and some include all North America in a new German-dominated world. These latter assume that the German Americans take over the United States as advance agents for Hitler.

If we assume Britain's defeat in the European war, what of British North America? Canada and Newfoundland are now at war with Germany. British refugees and perhaps even the British fleet might very easily flee there. It is inconceivable that the Canadians, who know that Uncle Sam must and will assist them if they are invaded, would surrender to Hitler. They have every reason to refuse his terms and rely on the United States to protect them. We are obligated to do so, not merely on account of our expressed promises, but to defend our vital interests. All or part of the British fleet may be forced to seek American bases. These vessels might anchor in Canadian ports for a while, but in the long run there is only one country in this hemisphere where they can obtain adequate repairs, out-fitting, and supplies — namely, the United States. British warships cannot even remain throughout the winter in the upper St. Lawrence without being frozen in the ice. If the British fleet transfers its permanent base to the Western Hemisphere, that base can only be the United States territory.

This will be an additional involvement for us in the present war. We could not refuse to receive such vessels without the risk of losing their co-operation. They might be sunk by their own crews. We cannot receive them without opposing Hitler and making it more certain that we should be part of new long-range hostilities.

If Hitler wins in Europe, we can assume that he will adopt a policy toward the United States designed to strengthen American appeasers, de-signed to discredit British sympathizers, to weaken the policy of any Washington administration, and to divide American opinion as deeply as he can. He might attempt all this in another Reichstag speech broadcast around the world. I can imagine Hitler saying something like this: —

Victorious Germany in the hour of its triumph offers the hand of friendship to all peace-loving peoples in the Americas. We have no desire to take a foot of American soil or interfere in any way with the domestic institutions of the American republics. We especially desire to live in peace and harmony with that great nation of forty-eight states which is bound so closely to us by the blood of twenty million of our own racial Germans. We have the greatest admiration for the history and the traditions of the United States. We admire the resolute independence of Washington, who struck off the bonds of the British conqueror from the American continent. Now we have successfully imitated the American example and made Europe free as well. From the beginning of the National Socialist movement we have recognized the great fundamental law of nature that free peoples living in the same regions of the world must work and plan together. Fate points the way to an American hegemony in the North American continent. This is the hour for the great American people to assume management of their own continental affairs. We do not propose to interfere in American policy, but will only welcome an expansion of the American people to their own natural frontiers. If the United States desires to assert its authority over those exploited and deluded peoples in the New World who have been so long oppressed by European empires, particularly by the British, we should accept this course as the fulfillment of a logical destiny.

It seems to me very likely that Hitler would adopt some such sort of generous and friendly tone toward the United States while he was consolidating his New Europe. He would overlook for the moment any hostile acts which we might have made and invite us to participate in the redivision of world territory. Hitler could place us in a very embarrassing position. If we extended aid, co-operation, and some form of control to former British, French, Dutch, and Danish possessions in this hemisphere, including, of course, Canada, Newfoundland, Greenland, the West Indies, and the Guianas, we should only do what our own military security demanded, but Hitler could make it appear that we were adopting a policy parallel to his own, and then he might, in a grand gesture, make us a present of territories which he was not able to possess himself. We should almost be forced to move in this direction, to assume responsibility for liquidating what was left of the war in North America.

We could be involved in a repatriation of German prisoners from Canada or Canadians held in Germany. We should be forced to make a sudden and perhaps unwelcome choice between a general policy of war toward the Old World, and entering into a complex series of negotiated agreements with Hitler covering a wide range of topics. We could not argue with Hitler; we would not submit to him. We could either fight him or negotiate with him. We might finally try to adopt a combination of both policies. I can imagine a situation arising somewhat in the form of a truce while prisoners were exchanged or other necessary formalities completed, but over the long future a general policy of undeclared war between our free world and Hitler's slave empire. Such a long-range hemisphere antagonism would bring with it a revolution in American policy, a reorganization of American economic life. It would tend to shatter our political and social institutions, and it would drastically revise our hopes for a fuller and freer existence. America would pass from a civilized era into a long night of siege.

3. *Economic Pressure*

In considering the economic pressure which
Hitler might apply to the United States through
third countries, let us briefly list various trading
areas of the world as they would appear after a
Nazi victory. In the Old World there would
probably remain but three such areas: the Axis,
covering Europe, Africa, and part of Asia; the
Soviet Union; and the Japanese Empire in East
Asia. These economic blocks all practise the
strictest of centralized trade control. They would
continue to deal with each other on the basis of
special bilateral agreements, covering specified
exchanges of commodities and services between
them. They would undoubtedly attempt to continue this system of trade with the countries of
the New World. Most of the Western republics
are now tied to the American economic system
through Secretary Hull's network of reciprocal
trade agreements.

Our system provides for most-favored-nation
treatment — namely, that when two of these
states complete an agreement, other countries
are granted the benefit of the lowered tariff rates,

provided they join in making similar agreements. It is impossible for us to include in our system states which continue to grant special favors to other states, for obviously they cannot admit us to equal treatment. In the same way those nations which have made special agreements with Germany by so doing promise to give the Germans special favors. No state in Latin America may at the same time be a member of the United States system of trade agreements and a member of the German bilateral trading system. A promise to enter the one network involves a promise to discontinue the trading methods practised in the other group.

Unfortunately for us, there are still several Latin-American countries which have remained outside our trade system. We have not been able to find room for them in it, because we are unable to make satisfactory arrangements for importing their commodities, many of which are directly competitive with United States products. This list includes notably cotton, grain, and packing-house products. Those countries, of whom the most important is Argentina, turn more naturally to the European market and will have no choice but to enter Hitler's system of bilateral agreements. This decision at once involves the stipulation that they do not conclude a trade agreement with the United States. It will lead to increased trade with Europe. As soon as this trade has reached the point where it is absolutely vital to Argentina and other Latin-American countries, the Germans will use their position of preponderance to insist that all trade with the United States be stopped, that American firms in those countries be closed down, and that American salesmen and business executives be sent home. These tactics are precisely the ones which Germany has successfully used in Eastern Europe for several years. The Nazis will force certain Latin-American nations to decide whether they will do all their business with Europe or none at all. In this way they may be able to create a trade block of several South American countries, particularly at the southern end of the continent.

Such nations can carry on a certain amount of trade among themselves and with the totalitarians. And we may be sure there will be considerable likelihood that this totalitarian trade area could expand to the northward, gradually pushing out our advance agents from one country after another. It might well include Argentina, Chile, Uruguay, Paraguay, and Bolivia. It might come to include Brazil, where two million Germans very nearly control the large coffee-growing state of São Paulo. Let us remember that Hitler would have the slave labor of the greater part of the world to work with. He could quote prices with which American firms could never compete. He could even afford to do business for nothing if necessary.

We know that the Nazis offered a few years ago to equip the forts of the Dardanelles with artillery free of charge, just to get German equipment used by the Turks. Over in this hemisphere, German planes have been carrying the mail free of charge in some parts of the Western Coast of South America, in order to cut out the service of Pan-American Airways. Does anyone imagine that private firms in the United States can stand up successfully against this type of subsidized competition?

Small nations the world over have tried in vain to protect themselves against such high-pressure dumping. I remember years ago when the

National Bank of Afghanistan approached me in order to obtain army trucks, ambulances, staff cars, and similar equipment. They preferred to buy from the United States at high prices rather than take Soviet materials which were practically a gift. I remember how the government of Abyssinia tried to interest American firms in constructing a radio station in Addis Ababa. They would rather pay market prices for our radio equipment than take cheaper Italian apparatus, staffed and serviced by Italian engineers. Both these little countries suspected that totalitarian powers had only military objectives in mind when they made apparently generous offers to supply goods cheaply. I well remember how the War Departments in Bulgaria, in Estonia, and in Lithuania tried to get me to interest American machine-tool manufacturers in building factories in those countries for the manufacture of machine guns, rifles, and anti-aircraft guns. It was not a question of price. They did not wish their countries' armament industries to be controlled by the Germans or the Soviets. But the lesson for us is this: They all proved to be helpless. They were all compelled in the end to submit.

4. *Arbitrary Nazi Methods*

If Hitler wins in Europe, he will control the Pope, the Vatican, the overwhelming majority of the Cardinals of the Catholic Church, and its central executive organization. He will be in a position to exercise pressure upon the Church through his power to confiscate schools, universities, orphanages, asylums, hospitals, monasteries, and other kinds of church property. The present Pope Pius XII was formerly Papal Secretary of State and before that Papal Nuncio in Berlin. He knows the Nazi system as few men have ever learned it. He is an accomplished scholar and diplomat, as well as head of the Church. I had the privilege of knowing him during his long residence in Berlin, and I am sure that he will do everything in his power to preserve the ancient liberties of Catholics living under the dictators.

But how far will the Catholic Church be able to protect itself? It has no weapons of force. Hitler is not open to reason or argument. He understands the logic of the sword alone. I fear that by the exercise of brutal pressure he can make the Pope an involuntary prisoner and hamstring church activities. What is the result going to be upon the great body of Catholics in the United States? For example, this country has been the largest source of funds for carrying on the work of the Church. If by a control of foreign exchange money is not allowed to be sent from the United States to Europe, what will happen to the structure of Catholicism? How will American Catholics feel if they are not allowed free access to the head of their religious community? Can Hitler and Mussolini by putting pressure upon the Church in Rome assure themselves that such pressure could be indirectly relayed to Catholic bodies on this side of the water — not only in the United States but in Latin America as well? Will the Catholic Church in order to save its European property and protect the lives of its leaders have to consent to a political compromise which would endanger our safety in so far as American Catholics follow their church? Would Hitler even go so far as to hold the Church up to ransom from the New World? These speculations raise alarming possibilities for the future.

In the year 1936 an International Lighthouse Keepers convention was held in Berlin. I was the

American delegate, although I had never even been in a lighthouse. This came about in order to save the amount of money necessary to send a real lighthouse keeper all the way to Europe. In the course of this convention an interesting bit of negotiation came up. It appeared that in this country we had developed an underwater radio signaling device which can operate between ships and shore or between two vessels at sea. This is extremely useful as a means of guiding ships into safe channels during storms. We attempted to secure permission to have such equipment installed in our merchant ships when they entered German harbors. The Germans refused because they also had the same type of signaling device in use in their navy, where it was particularly effective in transmitting messages to and from submarines. But their merchant ships were equipped with the device and could use it to receive weather and safety signals from the shore.

Now it proved impossible to install the apparatus in mid-ocean, so that American ships returning from Germany to this country could not be so equipped. But the German merchant ships entering our harbors would have the apparatus installed. The Germans saw no injustice in this arrangement which allowed them to use the device on both sides of the Atlantic while we were barred. This is the sort of treatment we should be likely to get from a victorious Germany after the war; only instead of merely involving harbors in Germany, it would mean the harbors of all the outside world. Instead of being confined to a signal device, such discriminatory treatment might cover almost every sort of regulation which ingenious and painstaking bureaucrats could apply to harass our citizens.

To show how arbitrary Nazi bureaucracy can be and how American business firms can be held up at the point of the Nazi gun, let us consider the sale of crude naphthalene. This product, prepared from blast-furnace gases, was a German monopoly when the Nazis came to power. The greater part of the sales were made to the United States, where it was used for the manufacture of mothballs and in dry-cleaning establishments. It was in the year 1934 that the Nazis suddenly stopped all shipments of naphthalene to this country and would not allow any more to be offered for sale. At the request of the American importers, I approached the German Ministry of Economics and told them that we desired to continue importation, as Germany was the only source of supply. After some time, the Ministry ruled that we could secure crude naphthalene in the future, provided the American companies interested would sign an agreement to purchase a fixed quantity each year for five years in advance, at a price which was three times the existing price at the time.

I informed the American importers of this ultimatum, and it was decided that we should make an energetic attempt to produce our own naphthalene in the United States. This was so successful that in a few years American manufacturers were offering naphthalene on the German market. We had become self-supporting and able to export our surplus. In this case Nazi arbitrary methods overreached themselves, but once Hitler controls the resources of several continents, he can make things extremely disagreeable for our business men by tactics of this kind.

CHAPTER V

THE UNITED STATES UNDER NAZI PRESSURE

1. Barter Agreements
2. Gangster Methods
3. Disorganization of American Business
4. State Socialism in America
5. America's Decisive Opportunity
6. Our Postwar Policy

1. Barter Agreements

AMERICANS who are concerned with the problems of postwar trade, and particularly those persons who believe that we might come to some sort of satisfactory trade relations with a victorious Germany, might study the *German-American Commerce Bulletin* of March 1941, published by the Board of Directors for German-American Commerce, 10 East 40th Street, New York. On page three appears a lead editorial, "German-American Relations at the Crossroads." Part of this runs as follows: —

Germany with a population of more than one hundred million people could easily buy from the United States each year three to four million bales of cotton, large quantities of wheat, lard, canned meat, fruits, copper, and a great variety of finished products, if reasonable and normal trade relations could once more be established between both countries. Will American wheat farmers, cotton growers, and fruit producers be given the opportunity to export again when the restoration of peace will leave most of Europe bare and in vital need of these essentials? . . . Today Germany is Europe, and thus the standard-bearer for the entire continent. Profound economic and social changes will follow in the wake of this development.

This quotation illustrates the theme of the whole publication. On the cover is printed a similar statement. On page eleven a picture of cotton in a Texas field illustrates our unsalable surplus of this commodity. These tactics are right in line with National Socialist instructions to German business men, issued in October 1934, and reading as follows: —

The pressure of the stocks of American raw materials shall be utilized and made to serve the purpose of enlarging German trade.

This is the same sort of propaganda which German business circles have been giving us for years.

Unfortunately for these hard-working German propagandists in New York, their same magazine contains on page twelve an official article sent over from Berlin and signed by Erich Neumann, Secretary of State in the Ministry of Economics — in other words, by one of the responsible heads of the Nazi government. This official, perhaps puffed-up with German successes and careless for a moment, blurts out the following statement of Germany's real economic aims:

All we wish to do is to make ourselves *independent of the outside world in the domains of foodstuffs and indispensable industrial materials.* All other products, particularly those we can do without in times of emergency, but which are a part of the standard of living to which a highly developed nation has a just claim, will continue to be obtained from foreign sources, in exchange for our own surplus production of manufactured articles. Independence in our war economy, but otherwise ready to contribute our proper share to international trade — that is the program which we strive to realize.

In other words, the National Socialist government intends after the war to maintain the policy they have already been practising before the war — to be self-sufficient in foodstuffs and industrial war materials. The Nazis have a mystical belief of linking German blood with German soil. They do not propose to purchase foods from us. The Food Ministry carried this policy to such extremes before the war that certain articles which were imported into Germany in small quantities from the United States were allowed to come in only if rendered unedible. Tallow is a good example. All edible tallow was strictly prohibited from entry. This import barrier on food was not 100 per cent perfect. A number of exceptions were made for special products from countries tied up with Germany; but with the increase of German territory through the war, it seems likely that the Nazis may approach their goal of self-sufficiency in food products.

Neither do the Nazis propose to import essential industrial war materials from abroad, least of all from us. In the light of this official standpoint, let's look back to the propaganda of our New York Nazis. How in the world can we expect to sell cotton, wheat, or copper when every one of these items is blocked out by the Nazis on the basis of national policy and when we know that before the war Germany was cutting down her imports on such products from this country as fast as possible? Such propaganda should not deceive any intelligent American who has had a chance to know the facts.

But someone may say that Secretary of State Neumann is willing that Germany import from us other products, "particularly those we can do without in times of emergency." These will be exchanged for Germany's own surplus production of manufactured articles. Just what products could be sold from the United States? Judging from my experience with the Nazi Import Control Offices, I think that these would, first of all, be essential tools and equipment for Germany's war machine, possibly some luxury goods, and certain articles which the Germans could buy in America much cheaper than anywhere else.

With foodstuffs and industrial war materials ruled out, what about our chances of selling manufactured goods? Well, to tell the truth, each of the twenty-five Import Control Offices in Germany has an advisory committee taken from German industry and trade. Most of these committees are headed by business men who are manufacturing articles which are usually competitive with American products. They have adopted a very consistent policy of keeping out foreign products which might hurt their own business.

Yes, but what did our trade before the war actually consist of, if all these kinds of goods were kept out? The answer: It was made up first of rush shipments of emergency war stocks and equipment, such as airplanes and parts, copper, petroleum, phosphates; and secondly of goods shipped in by American companies to their subsidiaries in Germany, in the hope that some day arrangements could be made to obtain payment. As a matter of fact, such latter goods were not traded to Germany — they were given. Of course, if we want to do more business like that — giving Germany something for nothing — I am sure the Nazis would usually oblige us by taking it.

Now, what about the possibilities of barter arrangements with victorious Germany after the war? Remember that according to the Nazis themselves, Germany is Europe. Could we barter with Europe? A great deal has been written and conjectured on this subject. Probably no American has had the opportunity to see as much negotiation for barter deals as I have.

I suggested to the American Chamber of Commerce in Berlin in 1934 that a special barter committee be set up, and this met regularly on Friday afternoons over a long period. We found numerous firms coming to us for aid, but they all wanted to get goods from the United States. Few firms came in with practical suggestions regarding German goods which they wanted to buy and which they could take to the United States and resell at prices that would show a profit. Such goods were extremely rare. One art dealer from Munich told me that he did have business of this kind. He sold Bavarian paintings in New York and had built up a quite satisfactory trade. He was so fearful that this business would be taken away from him by some greedy larger firms in Germany that he did not allow any payments to be made by check, for fear the German banks would find out too much of what was going on and try to steal his business from him.

It was my experience that the only successful barter negotiations which our American firms were ever able to conclude with Germany were small deals, averaging perhaps one to two thousand dollars apiece. These arrangements usually covered commodities which the firm produced or used itself and which were not for resale to others; but in this modern world it is rare to find the possibility of large business arrangements of this type. Seldom could we find a single American company which could exchange an article of its own manufacture for one from a single

German company which happened to manufacture some product that our firm wanted and
where the price of the goods on both sides proved
suitable. Usually, international trade occurs in
items which are for resale and not for use directly
by the importer. In cases where goods must be
resold, this simple type of barter fails to meet the
situation.

Not only that — the German government set
up rules and regulations for the conduct of
barter deals which made them almost impossible
as far as the United States was concerned. Since
Germany desired to reduce imports from the
United States and increase exports to this
country, the German government was unwilling
to allow barter deals with us at the straight ratio
of one for one — that is, an equal value of goods
exchanged. They insisted that the barter ratio
should be set at a minimum of one unit of
American goods in value and the balance in cash
against 1.3 units of German goods in value.

I do not happen to remember any deal which
we actually were able to work out at this
minimum rate. The usual barter ratio for our
ordinary commodities was set at three to one.
For example, American walnut growers tried to

arrange a barter of $100,000 worth of walnuts but found they would have to buy $300,000 worth of German burlap bags and barbed wire in exchange. This meant that the Association here would have to invest $200,000 in cash and hope to be able to recover this money by the re-sale of the bags and wire in the United States.

Such an arrangement makes trade practically impossible for American interests. Most of our firms know their own business better than any other business. Our walnut growers know something about selling walnuts, but very little of the market for burlap bags and barbed wire. If they succeeded in getting rid of their walnuts to Germany, they found themselves faced with the problem of getting rid of three times as large a quantity of unfamiliar German goods as the amount which they started to sell. No wonder the negotiations broke down.

In the case of manufactured articles which Germany was deliberately trying to keep out of the local market, the barter ratio was set at an even higher figure. On one occasion I pressed the German Ministry of Economics to give me the best terms on which they would allow American automobile companies to bring in cars and parts in exchange for German goods. The Ministry was reluctant to set any terms, but finally agreed that we could bring in cars and parts against German goods in the ratio of one to ten. In other words, an American automobile company which sold $100,000 worth of cars and parts would have to purchase $1,000,000 worth of German goods. This harsh ruling was obviously designed to show us clearly that Germany did not intend to take any more of our automotive products on any terms whatever, in spite of the fact that thousands of German car owners needed replacement parts for American cars imported into Germany before the Nazi era.

Of course, in any barter arrangement the German government insisted upon fixing the price, both of the American and of the German goods in question. The price set on German goods was usually the local price, naturally a high one on account of the high nominal exchange value of the mark and the amount of currency and credit inflation which has gone on inside Germany. The price set on the American goods was usually an arbitrarily low one and represented an attempt to beat us down. For example, I worked long and hard in 1937 in an attempt to barter

190

10,000 tons of West Coast prunes for an assortment of German products, but the German government would only allow a maximum price of three cents per pound for our prunes delivered in Hamburg. The deal, of course, fell through, because even the lowest-grade prunes were worth more than that on the Pacific Coast.

In order to save something from the wreck of their German holdings, many American companies have been forced to accept merchandise which was either unsalable, or so different from their usual line of business that they could hardly hope to put it on the market in this or other countries except at considerable loss. In this category come the 8,000,000 mouth organs which an oil company took in payment for petroleum, the 200,000 canaries which a manufacturing company got in exchange for a large press for making automobile bodies, and the live hippopotamus which a motion-picture firm took as part payment for motion-picture films.

Other firms have taken patents, participations, processes, and stock as part payment on unpaid bills; but there are still outstanding large sums, much of which probably means total loss. It is not as if the Germans were completely unable to pay their debts. For instance, the German government suspends interest payments on bonds held in the United States until the market price of such bonds falls to very low levels — such as five cents on the dollar. At that point the Germans quietly proceed to buy up the bonds. They are doing so even at the present time, and so profit by their own default. In the same way the German government has claimed to be unable to allow payment for American merchandise, shipped long ago to Germany, and unable to pay Americans the judgments which German courts have rendered in their favor, but it is quite able to finance propaganda in foreign countries and to produce military supplies and equipment for cash.

At the present time the German government is even trying to make some extra American dollars by selling to emigrants permission to leave Germany. Many American relatives of such hostages inside Germany have had the experience recently of being forced to pay tribute to the Nazis in various ways. One trick is to compel payment for rail and steamer passage to be made through the New York office of the Hamburg–America Line owned by the German government. This line, of course, has no ships running now between the United States and Germany, but collects a commission on passage money paid to it before turning the funds over to the American Export Lines, which actually carry the refugees from Lisbon to New York. It is often useless for American relatives to pay money directly to the American Export Lines, as then the Hamburg–America Line does not get its cut; and the German government refuses to release the refugees until their representatives here have had a chance to get their hands on some money.

2. *Gangster Methods*

There is no doubt that if Germany wins the war she will attempt more or less to standardize industry for all Europe and can hold out to individual firms the hope that their design might become the standard one for an entire continent or even for a Nazified world. Hitler can use prospects such as these as bait to tempt foreign business men to co-operate with him. Probably more important than such promises and inducements, though, are the threats that the Nazis

can use and the control which they now exercise
over the property of unfortunate firms in their
territory. Before the war started, most of our
smaller American companies had fled from Germany, abandoning such property as they had;
but larger firms with more extensive invest-
ments were hanging on desperately and sending
in good money after bad, because they could
hardly afford to give up their large holdings.

When we think that an American company
has been making more than half of all the passenger cars in Germany, that another is building the Red Cross ambulances for the army, that
still another has 20,000 filling stations, besides
other large properties, that a number of other
important United States firms have many millions of dollars invested in plant and equipment,
we can understand that they are peculiarly subject to pressure and threats from Nazi quarters.

Now the property of these firms and many
other firms in surrounding European countries
is affected. Supposing Great Britain falls and
other parts of the British Empire; this would
increase the pressure which the Nazis could put
upon American firms with property in such
areas. Look down the list of our large industrial

firms as quoted on the New York Stock Exchange. You will find almost every one has property abroad, if not in plant, then in distribution organization, patents, or stocks of goods. All this property is in danger of being used by Hitler as a hostage for the good behavior of the parent companies in the United States.

Some people express the fear that the Nazis may confiscate such American properties. This seems unlikely. They know a trick ten times as effective as that. They will allow the American holders to maintain their title to property in lands under Nazi control, but will subject them to threats of punishment and confiscation on the one side and promises and inducements for good behavior on the other. In this way, Hitler can be assured of plenty of points to apply pressure right inside the United States.

Of course, if he puts on the pressure too strongly, he will defeat his purpose. American companies are patriotic. They would not betray the interests of the United States under pressure, if the issue were clearly presented to them in that light — but it would not be. They would be asked to make only small concessions of policy at the beginning — for example to adjust their

personnel and advertising policies to bring them
more in line with German wishes.

One concession, if made, would inevitably lead
to another. The great trouble in dealing with the
Nazis is the fact that we never know their last
word. No matter how much you have agreed
to today, they will demand more tomorrow. The
experience of the Vichy government is an ex-
cellent illustration of this point.

In addition to the economic pressure which
Hitler can bring upon American companies, he
can bring individual pressure upon millions of
Americans who have friends and relatives in the
countries under his control. I have definite knowledge that numbers of such unhappy people are
afraid to state their true feelings regarding the
totalitarians, even though they themselves are
personally safe in the United States. They cor-
rectly fear reprisals against innocent persons
abroad and so dare not take a stand in this country
which their feelings and knowledge of the facts
warrant.

In October 1931, nearly one and a half years
before the Nazis came to power, Hermann
Goering expressed the desire to talk over economic
policies with a representative of the American

Embassy. Accordingly, I had lunch with him and talked until five o'clock in the afternoon. At that time, he gave me a warning to American business firms that they had better leave Germany. He explained that the National Socialist Party regarded the economic life of the country as a living organism, and that the presence of foreign firms inside their territory was like that of destructive bacteria in the human body — they set up an inflammation or irritation; and he said that, in due time, such firms would be forced to close their business and return home. In a friendly spirit, he asked me to warn them so that they might leave before getting into actual trouble.

Some years later, Walther Funk, then President of the Reichsbank and Minister of Economics, stated officially that in world trade after the war no private international trade would be permitted, that all trade must be between governments, as private transactions only lead to international anarchy.

Let me illustrate the difficulties of doing business with National Socialist Germany by relating the experience of an American firm making soft drinks. This firm, surprisingly enough, had a satisfactory business in Germany, the land of beer, for a number of years. After Hitler came into power, the company began to run into difficulties. German doctors certified that their product was injurious to health. The police reported that some of their buildings must be torn down, because they did not measure up to the Building Code.

After several experiences of this kind, the company approached me and said, "We understand that there is a way of arranging matters with the National Socialist Party Headquarters to keep foreign firms out of trouble. Perhaps you could help make an arrangement for us." I passed this word on to the Party Headquarters, and a few days later, a young man a little under thirty years, dressed in the party uniform, came into my office. He explained that he was the Propaganda Leader in the Province of Saxony and nothing would please him better than to assist the American company in their difficulty. "In fact," said he, "I am already helping seventeen other companies and would be glad to assist an eighteenth, particularly since it is an American concern."

"Just how is that arranged?" said I.

"The company should, first of all, appoint me as a member of their Board of Directors in Germany."

"Just how much would this cost?"

"Eight hundred dollars a month."

I began to see why this young Nazi enjoyed helping foreign firms and wondered whether he was doing equally well with the other seventeen. The company agreed to this proposal, and their troubles miraculously stopped for a while.

But this type of arrangement, while working well for short periods, is not satisfactory in the long run. It is an old experience that blackmailers always raise their price. So, after about two years, another Nazi official, superior to the friendly young man just described, and who apparently had not received a proper cut of the eight hundred dollars a month, made a new ruling — namely, that the product was Jewish and would pollute any pure Aryans that might happen to drink it.

The company came to me a second time. I suggested that we consult Dr. Robert Ley, head of the German Labor Front. Dr. Ley made the suggestion that a Nazi delegation visit the United States, at the firm's expense, in order to investigate whether the product was, in fact, Jewish. This was done, and an official report was duly prepared which certified that it could be enjoyed by the purest Aryans without any racial contamination.

Unfortunately, we had made the mistake of going right over the head of the official who had made the ruling in the first place. He was offended, and shortly came out with another ruling which stated that the beverage was not Jewish, but because it was foreign could not be consumed by any good Nazi. The company came back to see me a third time, and desired assistance. I thought this matter over for a long time and finally gave them advice which usually has to be given to any foreign firm that works long enough in totalitarian territory. I explained that there were several possible courses of action which a firm in their situation could take: —

1. They could approach the official in question and find out how much it would cost to have him change his ruling. It might amount to their profits for several years; but it would be worth finding out, at any rate.

2. They could close their German business and go back to the United States. That was the

course which I thought best under the circumstances.

3. A Nazi firm in similar circumstances might consider having the official assassinated.

Such are the usual alternatives which present themselves to business men who try to operate in a totalitarian state.

3. *Disorganization of American Business*

If we assume a Hitler victory over the Old World just how can we continue to conduct ordinary day-to-day relations between the hemispheres? Let us try to imagine how difficult this would be and some of the troubles that would arise for us. International relations are a complex affair. We touch the Old World at many points and through a variety of channels. Just how can we arrange the normal exchange of telegraphic messages over ocean cables when one end lies in a free country and the other is controlled by a totalitarian dictatorship? Shall we have to cut the cables, or can we set up some American government ownership or operation of our end of these lines to prevent Hitler from using them as a method of forcing an entry into our internal affairs? What shall we do about radio connections across the Atlantic? Can we allow our people to listen to insidious propaganda designed to break down our morale? Shall we have radio telephone connections with the Old World? Shall we radio pictures across the ocean? What arrangements shall we be forced to set up regarding the exchange of letters, second-class mail, including newspapers, magazines, and packages? Will it not be necessary for this country to have a censorship of mail at the frontiers? If we have to control foreign trade, as we surely shall if the Nazis win, shall we not have to control movements of foreign exchange? Will our government not have to open all first-class mail to see whether it contains currency? Shall we be able to have exchange of funds by money order with the totalitarian postal systems? It would not seem so, as they control all movements of funds through a central station and seize any foreign money coming in, no matter for whom it is destined.

Could we allow Hitler's newspapers and magazines to circulate freely in this country? He

202

would not allow ours to go to his subject peoples. Would we dare to permit American ships to visit the harbors of dictator-controlled countries? Our sailors and shipowners could not be guaranteed proper protection against arrest or the confiscation of property. Could we maintain consular and diplomatic officers in the New Europe? Would they be allowed to retain traditional privileges of extraterritoriality? Could our tourists travel abroad? What about the millions of people of this country who have close friends and relatives on the other side? What arrangements could be made for the exchange of Axis citizens here for American and Canadian citizens caught in the Old World?

What about the billions of dollars' worth of American property held in Germany or in the countries that Hitler has been taking over? What about the debts owed to American banks and bondholders by Germany and other European nations? If we are to be engaged in permanent hostilities with the dictators, all private interests must continue to suffer. But if we are to have a period of formal peace, some arrangements must be made to adjust these matters. They will prove extraordinarily difficult to settle.

We must not forget that the Nazis have long experience in this kind of negotiations. They have worked out new revolutionary methods of turning every one of these factors to their own advantage. We shall be fearfully handicapped if we allow individuals on this side to negotiate with a centralized bureaucracy on the other. Almost inevitably the United States government must extend its control over all matters of this kind in order to present a stiff front to the Nazi pressure. We shall have to change very many of our present practices. We could no longer allow American probate courts to pay out to totalitarian governments money bequeathed to individuals and institutions by wills. We could no longer allow the United States Veterans Bureau to mail every month millions of dollars in checks to our discharged veterans who are now living abroad. This money, of course, goes right into the pockets of the dictators, while the beneficiaries are paid off in different varieties of Hitler's phony currencies.

What arrangements would be necessary to take care of American patents registered in Europe? Under probable circumstances the owners here would get no royalties, nor would our authors and composers be able to collect anything in the way of royalties on copyrighted books, articles, and musical compositions used over there. Would we be willing to grant such rights to authors, composers, and patent owners of the Old World when we know that the money would go to the central government? Would we allow Hitler or his agents the right to appear in an American court to recover sums due from the people playing Strauss waltzes? Under the new setup Hitler would be the effective owner of the trade-marks of French champagne, Harris tweeds, and Copenhagen porcelain. He would control all stock of American corporations now owned anywhere in Europe. Could we let him vote that stock in our annual meetings? The impact of an immense totalitarian state through all these channels upon our economic life would be most dangerous and destructive. I feel that it would prove necessary for us to abandon at least for a time many of the liberties to which we have become accustomed. Our free economic society could not function under such a condition of external pressure in a totalitarian world. We could not allow American legal firms to represent the dictators without some sort of control by our authorities. We could not allow the liberty of the press, the mails, and of public meetings to be extended to foreign governmental agencies. This involves the censorship in our own country of activities which have been guaranteed under our Bill of Rights. We should have to suspend or amend our Constitution, creating a new bureaucratic system of control over the individual. We should undoubtedly be forced to have a Federal Police, fingerprinting everyone. We might even have to extend police power, requiring that every citizen report his movements, that every arrival and departure at hotels be reported to the nearest police station, as is done in Europe, and that an American equivalent of the Gestapo or OGPU be called into existence to combat actual or potential fifth-column activities. We should have to sacrifice a goodly portion of our treasured liberties in order to preserve a certain remnant of them. This is not a pretty picture.

4. State Socialism in America

If Hitler wins, we can expect our economic picture in the United States to be somewhat as follows: An expanded war industry which we must maintain and enlarge for the purpose of North America and hemisphere defense; a backed-up supply of certain exportable commodities, including cotton, grain, and tobacco, for which no market in the Western Hemisphere can be found; a growing shortage of certain critical materials, which up to now have been secured from the Old World. These shortages would not amount to much in terms of American dollars, but they might mean dangerous deficiencies in certain areas of our defense program and in the supply of many goods commonly used in the United States. We might, for example, have very little chrome. At the present time the automobile companies are requesting that when new chromium parts are ordered, the old broken parts be immediately sent back to Detroit in exchange. We might be seriously short of manganese, mercury, tin, antimony, tungsten, rubber, scientific instruments, optical goods, and other necessary commodities.

Our economy would be characterized by easy money, a nervous and depressed stock exchange, rising indebtedness, a high level of employment and wages in defense industries, and a feeling of dread regarding the future outlook. If Germany wins, our foreign trade will come almost to a standstill. At the present time two thirds of our foreign trade is with the British Empire. We have placed that proportion of our eggs in one basket. Hitler bids fair to smash both basket and eggs. Another large segment of our trade lies with Japan. If Hitler wins, he might take steps to integrate European and Asiatic trade, so that this market and source of supply would be suddenly taken from us. We should find an immediate drop in our business with the southern part of Latin America. What was left of our foreign trade would be only the portion which goes to North America and the Caribbean area. This restricted trade zone contains a large number of our good customers, but it would be impossible for them to absorb our customary total exports.

We have a carry-over of fifteen million bales of cotton, and we need to sell one half of our current crop to prevent further increase. If we cannot come to satisfactory trade relations with Hitler and the Japanese, we shall have to restrict the production of this commodity and find new sources of livelihood for a vast number of persons in the South. If Britain goes down, there vanishes our leading foreign market. Our other markets in the Old World have already disappeared. We shall have to revise our economy to take care of the workmen and industries now employed on sales to Britain and possibly Japan; we shall see a sudden contraction of our foreign markets for office equipment, machine tools, and other mechanical devices, petroleum and its products, copper and other nonferrous metals, miscellaneous items of iron and steel, chemicals, naval stores, canned, dried, and fresh fruits, not to mention many other items. We shall be forced either to trade with Hitler or to make a sudden readjustment of our economy which is bound to be painful and distressing to millions of Americans. Either choice involves us in acute difficulties.

Suppose we try to trade with Hitler. The American government must then commence negotiations in Berlin for some sort of exchange of commodities. We shall be handicapped at every turn because the Germans can put pressure upon factions and commodity groups in this country to secure larger shares of the deal for their own particular advantage. We shall not be able to interfere in the same way in Germany, because over there no one but the central government can conduct business negotiations with a foreign power except on pain of death. If the American government decides to negotiate, it may prefer to draw up only a covering agreement under which American interests could buy or sell with Berlin. If this is done, the Germans will out-trade us. They will use their united strength to force unfair concessions from individual groups in this country.

If, on the other hand, we conform to the Nazi pattern and conduct special negotiations between Washington and Berlin, covering commodities on a barter basis, we shall have to upset our whole economy as we know it now. This would put the American government directly into all sorts of trading enterprises. Our authorities here would have to swap stocks of American goods with the Germans at fixed prices, and then import the Old World equivalents and allot them in some manner to firms in this country. Just how can we maintain our system of free enterprise if our government is thus forced directly into all the deals which concern trade with the outside world? A quick result would surely be the introduction of fixed prices covering the imported commodities and those which we exchanged. This would lead to a forced allocation of commodities to private individuals and firms in the United States. We should be on a fair way to planned economy and a system of State Socialism.

5. America's Decisive Opportunity

This picture of the United States left alone in a friendless totalitarian world, forced to adjust its democratic economy under pressure from across both oceans, need never become a reality. We have still time — but not too much time — to intervene effectively and to reshape the future world along the traditional lines which have made us the happiest and freest people in the world. We still have a first, last, and only chance to win this war before it is too late. Hitler has not yet invaded Britain. If he could have done so in the spring of 1941, we can be sure he would never have moved his armies into the Balkans. Hitler does not know how to win quickly. All he can do is to pound away at the British Isles with his aerial forces and strive to destroy Britain's lifeline of shipping across the Atlantic. Such a campaign of attrition takes time. It gives the United States the all-important opportunity to unite, to arm, and to strike before it is too late.

Just what form of military intervention this country might take remains, of course, a technical problem for experts of our fighting services. Lindbergh has told us that we have no feasible plan for conquering Germany. Perhaps he imagines that our military problems should be discussed in the columns of the public press. Great military struggles have never in the past been decided according to precise plans. Wars must be fought as best they can, with circumstances as we find them. Many persons point to America's unpreparedness and assert that we are unable at this time to play any effective part in a world war. I suspect that many of these gentlemen might be opposed to our taking part in this war, no matter how well prepared we were. We have never been adequately prepared when the fateful hour of war arrived. Under our democratic system we may never be. We must prepare and fight simultaneously, as we have always done before.

It would seem that in the near future our most significant contribution to the war should be naval. With the assistance of part of the American fleet, we can guarantee the safe delivery of our war materials to the British Isles. But this would only be enough to deadlock the war, not to win it. Our next contribution could be an ever-increasing supply of bombers and fighting planes which can swarm over the heart of Germany's industrial regions, destroying land and sea communications, harbors, docks, factories, railway stations, and public buildings. We can smash the vulnerable factories for manufacturing ersatz materials. We can effectively cripple the huge German war machine by stopping its production of synthetic fuel and lubricants. We can destroy the plants manufacturing cotton and wool substitutes. We can prevent the Germans from securing adequate supplies of fats and vegetable oils. We can cause Hitler's machine to crumble by pulling out the pins at critical points. Only then, when the German army is starved, immobilized, and bewildered, will a final attack of mechanized land forces upon the Continent be necessary to clinch the victory.

This will take years, but the British as well as ourselves are far better prepared to stand a prolonged war than is Germany. Hitler boasted that his war preparations before September 1939 had already cost thirty-seven billions of dollars. He is spending nearly forty billion dollars a year now. Germany has looted her conquered neighbors and is consuming these windfalls of materials, but they can never be looted again; the supplies are gone. German economy is strained at every point. It is bound to smash sooner or later, if we keep up the pressure. How much sooner depends on when the United States openly enters the war. That day will mark the end of assurance and self-confidence in the ranks of the totalitarians. That day will see the beginning of a process of slow but sure disintegration.

Every German at heart thinks of three things as inseparably joined together — war, defeat, and inflation. The day we declare war will be the day the Nazis know they are beaten. They will continue to put up a strong resistance, but their hope of world dominion will be gone. Every one of them will secretly endeavor to escape the final defeat with as little personal loss and suffering as he can. Remember that Hitler needs time to organize his New Europe and make it contribute to his military machine. We must not give him that time. He shall not have it.

Remember that every nation conquered by the German armies makes one more area of discontent to be policed, that Hitler dare not withdraw from any conquered territory without danger of provoking revolution in other places. He must continue to advance and to win. He may conquer smaller nations, but he is not making any friends for Germany in the process. He will not be able to secure happiness or comfort for his own people in this way. The farther his armies advance to the south and east, the more responsibility he undertakes, the longer his lines of communication must be. The Germans could achieve their New Europe if they were once allowed to devote all their energy toward that end, but they can never do that if we keep up the military pressure from the West. History will record the story of one more would-be world conqueror who attempted too much.

We can win, but not in the halfhearted way we are now following. Theodore Roosevelt was eternally right when he said, "You can't fight half a war." A "short of war" policy now will leave us short of victory.

Lindbergh has warned us not to repeat the mistake the British and French made when they declared war in 1939. Just what was their mistake? Not in declaring war too soon, but at least three years too late. When Germany broke her treaty pledges to rearm, that was the time for action. Every year afterwards the cost of victory increased. If the Western allies had delayed still longer, does anyone believe they would have been better off in the long run? They would have been enslaved without having any real chance of defending themselves. The lesson for us is not to delay too long. We have been tardy in defense preparations. We must act more swiftly now, for that very reason. The sooner we declare war, the better for us. To wait is far more dangerous than to act.

If we are either unwilling or unable to fight with all our power to destroy Hitlerism utterly, we had better begin to prepare for the future by learning the German language, practising the goose step and the "Heil Hitler" greeting. We shall have thrown away the proudest position ever reached by any people in history, because we have lost the will to defend it in the only possible way. Attack is our best defense: attack at the heart of the enemy; attack with every resource of our vast, free, and vigorous American nation. Totalitarianism has grown until it now marshals the entire resources of a continent. But we too have a continent and a more productive one. The Nazis are strong in war, strong in organization. Even their economy is holding up much better than was expected. Yet they have a fatal weakness.

I have known literally thousands of Germans in government and private circles. I never met one who was fully confident of the success of the Nazi experiment. I never met one except Hitler himself who gave me the impression that he was so loyal to the Third Reich that he would cheerfully give his life in its defense.

The German people are still obedient, but not enthusiastic. They will follow Hitler as long as he seems to be victorious, but with their fingers crossed. If disasters come, if they face defeat, then the latent, hidden distrust will rise quickly to the surface. Then the moral defeats of the Nazi system will be felt in a widespread betrayal and repudiation of National Socialism.

The Nazis have taught the Germans to be selfish. They have been only too successful in such instruction. Their pupils and followers will one day callously abandon Hitler. I can well believe that the day may come when no German will admit that he ever was a Nazi or wore a brown shirt.

I remember a high German officer who pointed to the swastika on his uniform and said, "I have already sworn at different times to be true to death to three regimes — the Kaiser, the Republic, and Hitler. I wonder how many more different oaths of loyalty I shall have to take before my life is over."

6. Our Postwar Policy

In spite of the fact that peace looks very far away and that Hitler's machines are still crushing opposition in various parts of the Old World, we should look ahead to the postwar period in order to discuss possible solutions and prepare ourselves for them. Every day that goes by increases the relative importance of the United States in world affairs. No matter what we intend to do, it will be important for the rest of the world. It may even be decisive. As the war looks now, and in thinking a long way ahead toward a final world settlement, it seems to me that there are only two alternatives. There is no use for us to consider a stalemate or a regulated peace. To me that would mean only a short breathing space until Hitler could make ready for his final victory.

You see, I do not believe that the Nazis are organized for peace at all, or would know what to do with it if they got it. I think their system is a more or less permanent state of war, with only short periods of preparation between conflicts. Nor do I believe there is any use in counting on an unaided British victory in the present war. There will be none. We may admire the British, but there are too few of them. Their industries are too small, their resources too widely scattered, to achieve victory over a continent dominated by the most ruthless, scientific, and masterful dictator that the world has ever seen. This leaves us two alternative settlements for a future world — a German settlement or an American settlement. I furthermore do not feel that it is necessary for us to plan very extensively regarding the future world order in the event of a German victory. No one would then take any notice of our plans. Hitler will have plenty of plans of his own. We would not be invited to the peace conference; in fact, if Hitler wins, there will be no peace conference and no peace treaty. The Germans will simply mop up their enemies and set up their rules and regulations for the guidance of subjugated peoples. What would be the use of a peace treaty with Hitler when everyone knows that he can tear up treaties just as fast as he signs them?

Now, on the other hand, there is the possibility of an American victory after a very long-drawn struggle. I say American victory because the Americans' share will continually increase as the war goes on. That is, it will have to if our side is to win. If our share does not increase above what it is now, Hitler will win.

In thinking about the postwar world, after an American victory, we must imagine Europe almost completely stripped of peacetime production, her peacetime industries shattered, worn-out from years of effort without installation of new equipment, and blown to bits by aerial bombs and land artillery. Daily the British and German air forces are tearing out the vitals of each other's industrial fabric. When the Germans bombed Coventry they smashed the city that made bicycles for the British Empire. The

British came back to bomb Gelsenkirchen, the center for making German mining equipment. The Germans then took revenge by destroying a large part of Birmingham, the center of the hardware trade. The British then bombed Hanover, which made tires and other equipment for the Continent. If this sort of thing goes on for several years more until we win, neither the British nor the Germans, nor probably anyone else in Europe, will be equipped to meet the postwar requirements for ordinary needs, let alone the great task of physical reconstruction.

Only one great country will possess the mechanical equipment, the raw materials, the finances, and the energy to rebuild a postwar world. America alone will have the strength, the resources, and the leadership which are needed. Our very name is potent in Europe. Europeans may sometimes sneer at Americans, but they do in their hearts acknowledge that we possess a disinterestedness and a generosity which they have never been able to show. Of course, we can give evidence of this attitude. We must maintain it, we must exceed our efforts in the last war crisis if we are not to have a whole series of destructive wars.

As I see it, it will not be possible — win, lose, or draw — to return to the old system of private trading and laissez-faire economy which was supposed to exist up to 1914. This was never really reconstituted after the First World War. The impoverished nations after that war turned to increased political control over economic forces. Governments entered the business field at almost every point. They will do it again; they are doing it now. Whether we like it or not, our whole system of comparatively unregulated free enterprise is temporarily in eclipse, and will not return during our lifetime. I do not say that with any satisfaction — I regret it. But I believe in facing the fact. The world, after the present war, will be a world of regulated economic life. We shall have bargaining between labor and capital, bargaining between agriculture and industry, bargaining between business and government, and bargaining between nations. The first and most pressing problem of the postwar period will be to secure a bare minimum of existence for populations living under the most difficult privations. Actual improvements in conditions will come slowly. The great choice in postwar economics will lie between a world of nationally regulated economics and some form of international co-operation, federation, or regulation. New types of international institutions must be created. Some of the old ones have failed. Few people believe that the League of Nations could be re-created as it was. On the other hand, most informed persons would agree that the International Postal Union and International Labor Office have done valuable work and ought not to be discontinued. Some measure of international co-operation must exist. We shall not scrap our merchant shipping or dismantle our long-distance, short-wave radio stations, and most of our largest cities will remain on the seacoast. Why are they there? For trade with the outside world, of course.

A continuance of economic nationalism, reinforced by the new high-pressure tactics which the totalitarian states have worked out, is very possible. It is too likely to happen to suit me. The passions unleashed by war, the hatreds and fears of a hungry, disillusioned world, create national antagonism and national barriers. It must be plain that after this war there will be more hate, less trust and confidence, and more suspicion, less friendship. After this war it will not be a case of getting the lambs and the lions to lie down together. The lambs will be mostly all devoured. There will only be well-armed but torn and angry lions left. Nevertheless, they must cooperate — they must trade or die. A revival and extension of economic nationalism after this war is a certain guarantee of bigger and better wars to come. It will prove that we have learned no more from World War No. 2 than we did from World War No. 1. It will postpone the final coming of peace and order indefinitely. I say with conviction and emphasis that we can never expect to see real, lasting prosperity again until a decent measure of international co-operation is established.

This is going to cost us a great deal. First of all, it will cost a great deal of money. But we have the money. We have now about 90 per cent of all the gold in the world. Most of it is the property of the United States government. It was sent here largely in payment for our export commodities. Our gold and silver can be used as a basis for international currencies, linked to the American dollar and supervised by some sort of international control in which the United States must have a leading voice. If we are unwilling to use our buried stores of precious metals in this way, we might as well throw them away. They serve no other useful purpose, and we have been gypped in exchanging our goods for them.

Some people may say that we have enough government indebtedness already without making larger commitments to finance the outside nations. I say that even if we lost all this money we should be no worse off than we were before. We must finance our impoverished customers in order to keep business operating. It is better to lose money occasionally in business than to have no business at all. We would have gained more in the past if we had kept on financing Europe after 1929 rather than being forced to spend all the billions which are now going into the defense program. If we are wise, generous but not gullible, enterprising but not greedy, we can rebuild this war-torn world. We want to give employment to our own people, to maintain our price level, expand our world trade, create thousands of interesting and well-paid jobs for Americans in foreign countries; and all this will cost us only one thing — increased effort. After all, that is what we want. We all desire interesting, stimulating, well-paid employment. We Americans do not desire to stagnate and allow our machines to rust. We like activity and enterprise. We shall have nothing to lose in such a program, and, in very truth, a world to gain.

But this postwar reconstruction leadership by the United States will cost us more than money, of which we have plenty, and effort, which we enjoy. It will cost us the sacrifice of some of our dearest prejudices and opinions. That will really be painful. We must grow up, abandon our old colonial-mindedness, and be willing to take part — the greatest part — in postwar reconstruction. This may involve risks and loss, but none of them so great as the risk and the loss if we do nothing and withdraw unto ourselves. We must be pleased to see other peoples grow strong and prosperous on account of our support. We must not begrudge the success of others. We must not worry particularly if the rest of the world is not as grateful as we think they should be. The rich and strong man must learn not to expect gratitude or affection. It is enough for him if the world is prosperous and contented, and he knows that he has more to gain in the long run from such a state of affairs than the poor man.

We must adopt as a nation the philosophy of

our successful business men. They understand how to take risks, how to cut losses, and then forget them. They do not cherish grudges against their dead-beat customers. They write them off the books, charge it to profit and loss, and go after more business. We had the right idea in our period of postwar expansion in the boom years. Only we loaned too quickly, too indiscriminately, and without supervision and control. Then when things began to look black in 1929, we stopped loaning and wanted our money back. That was just the time when we should have put in more money. We proceeded at too fast a pace in the boom years, and drew back just when the world needed our financial support most of all.

Some people still begrudge the loans that we made to the outside world from 1921 to 1929, but remember we had eight years of prosperity. We increased our own production and our national income many times more during this period than the total amount we lost. Eight years of prosperity were worth much more than all our defaulted loans together. America is a productive country, in agriculture, raw materials, and industrial products. Exports from our highly efficient economy flow naturally to other parts of the world. It is much more difficult for us to balance them by imports which we really can use and which minister to our comfort and satisfaction. We can export again if we will finance the world in a big way. We shall have losses, but good management can minimize them.

The bees work busily all summer and store their hives full of honey. The farmer takes some of the surplus honey and uses or sells it, but this does not hurt the bees. They still have plenty to live on through the winter; and they are happy next year, for they have empty hives to fill again. In the same way America is more happy and prosperous when its industry is humming; everybody has a job, even if some of our exports are consumed by bad debtors abroad. The main thing is to keep the machinery turning, keep the level of production and consumption high. Our experience in the inter-war period should help us do a more satisfactory job this time.

We must not worry lest some foreign nations may gain proportionately more than we do from postwar reconstruction. We must be more interested in the fact that we gain ourselves, rather than lose. We must not worry unduly about the British peace aims; by the time this war is over, the chief British aim will be their aim to please us. Right now we could undoubtedly secure the British assent to any and all peace proposals that we had in mind. The more difficult task is for us to make up our minds what kind of postwar world we wish to see, and how we are going to create it. No one is going to prevent us; we shall be elected to this task by a unanimous ballot. We must perform it — not to save the world, but to save ourselves.